MW01028166

The Case Against Spanking

The Case Against Spanking

How to Discipline Your Child Without Hitting

Irwin A. Hyman

Jossey-Bass Publishers • San Francisco

Substantial discounts on bulk quantities of Jossey-Bass books are available to corporations, professional associations, and other organizations. For details and discount information, contact the special sales department at Jossey-Bass Inc., Publishers (415) 433–1740; Fax (800) 605–2665.

For sales outside the United States, please contact your local Simon & Schuster International Office.

Jossey-Bass Web address: http://www.josseybass.com

 Manufactured in the United States of America on Lyons Falls Turin Book. This paper is acid-free and 100 percent chlorine-free.

Library of Congress Cataloging-in-Publication Data

Hyman, Irwin A.
　　The case against spanking　:　how to discipline your child
　without hitting　/　Irwin A. Hyman.
　　　p.　　cm.　—　(The Jossey-Bass psychology series)
　　Includes bibliographical references and index.
　　ISBN 0-7879-0342-6 (pbk.　:　alk. paper)
　　1. Discipline of children.　2. Corporal punishment.　I. Title.
　II. Series.
　HQ770.4.H96　1997
　649'.64—dc21　　　　　　　　　　　　　　　　　　　　　　96-51872

FIRST EDITION
PB Printing　　　　10 9 8 7 6 5 4 3 2 1

Contents

To Julia

I gave you a mother who will never hit you.

Preface

There is no sense in telling you this is a neutral, completely objective book about spanking, otherwise known as corporal punishment. First, I don't believe that anyone in our culture could write such a book. Second, in 1969— during my third year as a teacher in a small rural elementary school—I decided that children should never be hit by adults, and I have believed this ever since. My conclusion was based on a review of the extant research on discipline, personal reflection about the meaning of hitting children, and observations of too many excesses. It took another ten years before we, as a nation, began to recognize that many of those excesses were abuses engendering long-lasting emotional damage both to children and to the parents who abused them.

A significant part of my professional work has focused on discipline. I believe, and I hope to convince you, that there is absolutely never any reason to hit a child or adolescent. Now don't tell me that this "radical" belief is rooted in my fuzzy thinking and my liberal, ivory-tower mentality. If you really believe that, try working as a therapist, consultant, and educator for thirty years with angry, hostile, and sometimes violent kids and their parents and teachers, as I have. And don't tell me that "all those kids need is a good swift kick in the behind." How do you think most of them got to be so angry, hostile, and violent in the first place? By gentle, reasoned, loving, and informed parenting and teaching? Not any kid I ever worked with!

So, if you are a hard head on this topic, forget this book. If you don't want to listen to reason, feel free to stop here. I'm not going to threaten you with a good beating if you don't read my book, and even if I could, I doubt that would convince you that hitting kids is just a bad idea. You would be so angry that I hit you and then forced you to do something you really didn't want to do that you wouldn't agree with anything I said. Get the point?

Despite my admitted bias, everything I say in this book is based on extensive research, ample clinical experience, and observations of a wide number and variety of discipline situations. I will convince you of my position by telling you about the many negative results of our country's dedication to and belief in the effectiveness of punishment to solve individual and societal problems related to misbehavior and delinquency. I will convince you that we all pay dearly for those who believe that what most "bad" kids need is a good whacking.

If you read this book, you can learn, without psychobabble and fancy statistics, about the research on discipline that I and my colleagues have reviewed and conducted. I will share with you my experience as a therapist and parent and tell you about the many ways that other parents and whole cultures have dealt effectively with misbehavior without ever thinking about hitting children.

And don't tell me that you have been hit and it didn't do you any harm. Or as a number of legislators have told me, "I was spanked when I was a kid and look where I am now." Some even claim that they might have turned out to be criminals if their parents hadn't given them a good licking when they deserved it. I will answer these inanities and all the others in due course.

When I first became known for my work in school discipline, I received frequent requests to debate the issue of corporal punishment on talk shows. I will never forget my first major experience, about twenty years ago. I was invited to the studio in New York City for the show.

I was quite nervous and was barely able to present my arguments against hitting kids when a vitriolic female caller laid me out. After a few calm words she worked herself into a frenzy. Not only did she claim I didn't know what I was talking about but she blamed me and my "kind" for ruining this country. She claimed that we should return to the good old days when children respected their parents and teachers. She went on to recount that in her early years of growing up as one of eleven or so siblings in Ireland, she learned what respect really meant. When they misbehaved, not only were they spanked, they were made to kneel on dried peas and assume a posture of praying for forgiveness for their sins!

I was stunned by the vehemence of the majority of the callers who had a field day accusing me and all other child psychologists and fellow travelers of poisoning the minds of American parents. Somehow, we were the Commie, pinko, liberal elements in our society that fostered permissiveness so that our country would lose the cold war.

A Shift in Popular Opinion

Well, the times they are a'changing. I and my ilk have produced massive amounts of research and clinical evidence to demonstrate the advisability of programs of discipline that are both humane and effective. They don't rely on fear and pain. Many people now realize the link between spanking, hitting, beating, and child abuse. Many parents have taken courses in positive parenting and have learned alternative methods of discipline. Many of us have gained experience with the media and have effectively convinced parents and policymakers that hitting in both homes and schools is a bad idea.

Now shows like *Oprah* and *Geraldo*, where I have appeared on multiple occasions, can't seem to find mainstream educators to debate me on school paddling. Other than those who base their arguments on their interpretations of the Bible, few well-known, credentialed parenting experts will appear to defend the practice on national TV. In addition, the callers on talk shows who oppose corporal punishment tend to outnumber those who favor it.

Parental Versus School Spanking

There are many more "experts" who think they have the data to support parental spanking than there are who support school paddling. While this book will speak to school spanking, much of what I have to say here addresses the issues of parental spanking. Now, of course, I refer to parents spanking their children and not to someone spanking parents, although in some cases I can think of some strong justifications for a good thrashing of some parents who seem to think that is the only way to stop someone from doing something that is wrong. In any event, the underlying issues and solutions to misbehavior in any setting are pretty much the same, so at times the two will be intertwined. Now, before we turn to the first chapter, let me give you a little background.

Challenging Conventional Wisdom

In 1976, with support from a number of national organizations, I started the National Center for the Study of Corporal Punishment and Alternatives (NCSCPA; at that time we called it National Center for the Study of Corporal Punishment and Alternatives in the Schools) at Temple University. At that time, only New Jersey and Massachusetts forbade teachers to paddle schoolchildren. Having been a student and teacher in New Jersey, I knew that children could be educated without hitting them. Yet many American educators, parents, and citizens labored then, as they do now, under the assumption that sometimes the best route to a student's mind is through his behind. At that time, I naively assumed that within ten years we could sufficiently demonstrate to educators, parents, and the public the inherent paradoxes in that and other witty aphorisms about corporal punishment in schools. In fact, I stated as much—to the amusement of the senior members of the

NCSCPA board of advisors, who were more familiar than I with the battle I faced.

The board members, representing such groups as the American Psychological Association, the American Orthopsychiatric Association, the National Education Association, and the American Civil Liberties Union, were amused because most were seasoned warriors in the battle against corporal punishment in schools. They were well aware of Americans' penchant for paddling, swatting, spanking, and "whuppin" children in schools and in homes.

In 1976, I did not consider myself an expert on corporal punishment in schools or in the home. However, I soon discovered that almost everyone else in the universe considered himself or herself an expert. Why? Because almost everyone has either been spanked, observed someone being spanked, read about it, or heard or saw it in the media. I quickly discovered that most Americans whom I encountered were deeply and emotionally enmeshed in their beliefs whether they were for or against spanking. In fact, I found few people to be neutral on the subject, but lots who just knew that bad behavior deserved a good swat on the derriere.

These deeply held beliefs about what to do when children misbehave, based on personal experiences, religious assumptions, family and regional patterns of child rearing, and political orientation, needed to be challenged. But the challenge had to be based on research and facts rather than emotion and personal anecdotes. It also had to be based on sound and effective alternatives to hitting children to get them to behave. And what a challenge that has been.

Looking Toward Alternatives

Many people would like to believe that discipline is pretty simple. You simply say to the child, "You do as I say or you get hit. I am the parent (teacher) and I set the rules. The more you break the rules, the more I hit you. Period. End of discussion!"

Although this punishment-based dialogue may be effective in a variety of situations, the real reasons children misbehave are much more complex. That is why the challenge involves three prongs. First, you most convince people that the threat and use of punishment, and especially corporal punishment, causes more harm than good. At the same time, you have to teach people about the many proven, positive, and effective alternatives *to* punishment—rather than alternative punishments—that is, about methods of prevention and treatment of misbehavior. Finally, you have to help people understand that when punishment appears necessary, it should be relevant and effective and should not involve the infliction of physical or emotional pain. Alternative types of punishments include time-outs, withdrawal of privileges, and the possibility of restitution. Even though I agree that sometimes punishment or at least the threat of it appears necessary, I sometimes regret that part of the title of the NCSCPA uses that "A" word. Why?

Too often people conceptualize discipline in terms of punishment. For instance, during a workshop in Indiana with school administrators that was titled Corporal Punishment and Alternatives, one of the participants accused me of dishonesty because the workshop didn't focus on punishment alternatives to paddling.

As I write this book in the summer of 1996, twenty-seven states and most city and suburban schools in the country either ban corporal punishment or rarely use it. We have come a long way and may someday join almost all the other Western democracies (Canada and parts of New Zealand and Australia are the only others that allow corporal punishment in schools). Although the battle is far from over, it is now time to begin a concerted effort to address the issue of parental spanking and also tie it to school spanking.

It is clear that widespread acceptance of school corporal punishment in any region of the country mirrors commensurate acceptance of hitting in homes. You can't separate the two. In two previous books, *Corporal Punishment in American Education* and *Reading, Writing and the Hickory Stick*, I have addressed school corporal punishment in detail. Both books offer sufficient references and scientific backing to satisfy most skeptics. The purpose of this book is to focus more on parental spanking and to offer a very readable format.

This book is dedicated to the proposition that hitting children should not be acceptable in any setting and to offering positive alternatives. I will talk about both school and home issues and focus on solutions to common discipline problems that many people believe require the use of spanking. Although I base my arguments on scientific and clinical evidence, I want to assure you that as a parent I never spanked my own children. I know plenty of other parents who have not spanked their kids. Their kids and mine have turned out just fine. You can do the same.

Acknowledgments

Before I begin, I want to acknowledge the help of some people who made this book possible. First, Barbara Hill went beyond the call of duty as editor, adviser, and coconspirator in helping me to conceptualize and write this book. Theresa Erbacher, who will be an outstanding school psychologist when she completes her doctoral studies, was invaluable in helping me meet the deadline for completion of the book. She helped with typing, organizing, editing, and keeping me on track. I also want to thank two more of my students, Joyce Spangler and J. J. Stafford, who contributed material on spanking bans in Europe, and Mary Stewart and Leo Thomas for their compilation of information about the Michael Fay case and Singapore. Finally, I would like to thank Mary Lampman and Dawn Studzinski for their contributions to this project.

January 1997   **Irwin A. Hyman**
                                                Temple University

The Case Against Spanking

1

An Alien Point of View

You may remember the popular sitcom *Mork and Mindy,* which will probably resurface periodically on Nickelodeon as long as that children's channel survives. In this sitcom, Mork is an alien who reports back to his superiors each week about the human condition. To my knowledge, he never spoke about disciplining kids. If he did, or in fact if any alien anthropologist were to describe the ritual we call spanking, it might sound something like this:

Strange Rituals in the Supermarket

MORK: Nan-noo nan-noo, Mork calling Orson, come in Orson.

ORSON: Yes, Mork, what new and striking information do you have to report about the earthlings?

MORK: Well, after being here several months, I realize that I have been behind in noticing a peculiar child rearing ritual that was smack right in front of me. It's a really strange ritual that many American earthlings perform with their children. They actually hit their own offspring. Not only that, they let strangers, called teachers, hit them with wooden paddles. The ritual includes verbalizations by the spankers like "this will hurt me more than you," "I am doing this for your own good," "when you grow up you will thank me for hitting you," and "I am hitting you because I love you."

These statements are filled with concepts that earth people might call paradoxes, oxymorons, or hypocrisy. I'll tell you a little more about this in a minute.

Now, I haven't directly observed these contradictory statements while parents are hitting their kids because most spanking is done in private. But I have often watched public spanking rituals at the institutions where parents purchase food, called supermarkets.

Parents take their young earthlings between about one and three or four years of age to the supermarket. The food is on shelves along long aisles, often within reach of the young children. The first part of this ritual is kind of a contest. The parents' part is to move along quickly enough to get the ritual over, while at the same time observing the items needed on the shelves and getting them into a cart. They must also make sure the child, or children, don't grab, consume, destroy, or throw the items to the floor or at other parents and children. Often these other parents are attempting to maneuver in the opposite direction in the small amount of space allowed for the two carts to pass.

As parents pass through this first part of the ritual, speed and agility are generally the determinants of success. The parent usually wins. But parental speed and agility don't seem to help much in the second and more difficult half of the ritual—the checkout line. The supermarket managers have designed a sort of narrow chute through which the parents must push the cart, stop it, and then unload it. Within easy reach is a seemingly endless supply of all types of candies, chewing gum, and nifty little toys that are highly desirable to young earthlings.

After having endured the first part of the ritual without gain, the children are frustrated and angry. Here is a typical scenario:

Kid: "I want that."

Parent: "No, Jimmy, you can't have it."

Kid: "I want it."

Parent: "I said, you can't have it. I will give you some of that kind of candy when we get home. We have plenty at home."

Kid: (*Starts to scream and cry.*) "No. I want it now!"

At this point, the parents begin to look around to see who is staring at them and feel an increasing need to do something to save face.

"Parent: I said no. When I say no, I mean it. Now stop screaming."

Kid: "Whah! Whah! Whah!"

Parent: "OK! You asked for it."

MORK: Then the parent smacks the kid on the wrist, hand, or behind. This appears to be the signal for the child to cry harder. I really don't understand this part. The parent tells the kid to stop crying and screaming or the kid will get hit again. But that seems to make the child cry even more!

ORSON: I think I understand. This whole ritual is a matter of control. Manager and kids are in control of the parents. They make the parents buy things that the parents don't really want. So the kids know they will get spanked, but they also know they will get what they want. But sometimes they must just want to get spanked. It all seems very strange and messy, as confusing as what you have been telling me about human love.

MORK: You are right, oh wise one. For instance, the other day I asked Mindy about it. I said, "What a strange thing to do! You earthlings tell your offspring that you love them and then you inflict pain on them. Then you tell them that the reason you cause them pain is because you love them so much. You call this punish-ment, but you also punish criminals, deviants, and others who break the law. Sometimes policemen hit them. Does that mean that policemen also love criminals? Some criminals inflict pain on their victims. Do the criminals love their victims too? This is all very difficult to understand."

ORSON: Does any of this have to do with training kids for adult lovemaking?

MORK: This part is really weird. I found out that the nerves of the behind, the place on children's bodies that gets spanked most, are also hooked up with the nerves that go to the sexual organs. Parents give kids a pain in the behind by spanking them and then say that they love them at the same time. I think some kind of bonding takes place. From what I have read, some kids seem to get a sexual reaction when they are spanked hard. When these kids grow up they love to get punished as part of their sexual rituals. They call it bondage.

ORSON: You mean bonding and bondage are the same?

MORK: I am not sure. But this is the only way I can explain why some people need to get spanked in order to make love. Well, I will try to find out more about that ritual for my next report. Nan-noo nan-noo. Mork, signing off.

You don't have to be from another galaxy like Mork to realize that we have some strange beliefs and practices associated with hitting children. If you could disengage from your own childhood and examine spanking from an alien's point of view, you might ask some of the same questions that Mork asked.

And there have been people with that kind of alien point of view much closer to home. On the North American continent, when the white people arrived, there were both peaceful and warrior cultures that did not endorse hitting children. Their leaders were shocked when they observed white men hitting children. There is a story of a great Nez Perce Indian chief who was on a peace mission to meet with an American general. While riding through the settlement he observed a soldier hitting a child. The chief reined in his horse and said to his companions, "There is no point in talking peace with barbarians. What could you say to a man who would strike a child?"

As we were indoctrinating Native Americans with Western theology and concepts of childhood, we convinced those who survived the white man's largesse to thoroughly beat the devil out of recalcitrant youth. Our gift of alcohol further enhanced the frequency and severity of spankings, which escalated to beatings. Now tribes that historically never hit children have high rates of child abuse. Does that help you get the connection between the mere cultural acceptance of hitting children and eventual escalation to abuse? But more on this later. For now, within the context of discipline, let us define exactly what we are talking about.

Discipline, Punishment, and Corporal Punishment

When a father says to his son, "Keith, if you don't do what I told you to do, you will get a good smack," it is clear to both parent and child that Dad means to punish Keith if he doesn't comply. Most observers would call this an example of discipline in action. But what if Dad says, "Keith, I am really proud of you for not hitting your little brother when he cursed at you." Most people would not recognize that Dad is practicing positive discipline by praising Keith for his self-control or self-discipline. Let's examine what we mean by discipline, punishment, and corporal punishment.

Discipline

Ask any American to define discipline and the most likely response will be that it is punishment. For many, punishment means spanking, the most common form of punishment of children in America. Yet the term discipline comes from the Latin, *disciplina,* which had to do with learning and teaching. It is also rooted in the concept of the disciple. Disciples are those who willingly and without coercion follow and emulate their mentors, teachers, or gurus. Neither term implies coercion, force, or punishment.

Now, this is not meant to be an opus on political science, but I think it is important to understand where we come from when we talk about discipline. After all, we have all been disciplined from birth. As infants, we were disciplined about when we could suckle, when and what we could eat, and when and where we could eliminate. As we matured, we were disciplined about our language, our behavior, and our religious beliefs. Rules and punishments still emanate from legislatures, courts, police, and employers. Because we have all been disciplined all of our lives, most of us think of ourselves as experts on the topic. Just ask anyone on the street what he or she thinks we should do with delinquent kids or adult criminals. Most people have strong opinions about child discipline, crime and punishment, sentencing and jails, and what to do about violence in our society. But many so-called experts on all these discipline-related issues falter when they find that they can't discipline their own children.

There are many types of discipline, but they all have the intent to persuade or force someone to act in a particular way. Every society has values, standards, and models regarding how citizens should behave. Usually, these values and their enforcement are determined by the leaders' political orientations, religious beliefs, and institutional structures. How societies enforce rules often depends on beliefs about human nature and conceptions of childhood and children. Most contemporary societies can be placed on a continuum between authoritarian and democratic orientations.

Truly authoritarian societies emphasize unquestioning loyalty to leaders, reflexive obedience to authority, and the foolishness of dissent. Children are taught at home and school that they must not question requests by authorities, including parents, and that punishment will invariably follow disobedience. Males dominate the society, essentially owning their wives and children. Everyone recognizes the immediacy and possibility of the use of physical force to make people conform. Physical and mental coercion are the mainstays of authoritarian discipline.

True democracy is based on humanistic ideals and beliefs. To confirm this about American democracy, look at the Declaration of Independence. Underlying that document is the assumption that each citizen, and by implication each child, has a God-given right, guaranteed by government, to pursue happiness.

Our founders recognized that children must learn shared responsibility to others, but they saw the cornerstone of responsibility as self-discipline, not discipline by coercion. They understood the potential harm of a tyranny of the majority, therefore each child was recognized as unique and deserving of the right to develop that uniqueness. Combining contemporary scientific knowledge about discipline with the philosophical foundations of democracy is not difficult. Democratic discipline in the home requires that children should be taught to do the right thing because it is the right thing to do. This is called *moral persuasion*, as opposed to *moral coercion*, which is based on fear of punishment. For instance, Johnny must learn not to hit his sister because it hurts his sister, not because he is afraid of getting caught and being spanked. Because he knows what it feels like to be hurt, he will eventually control his behavior by empathizing with others who are hit. Of course it takes more time and patience to teach this lesson, but it is one that becomes internalized for life.

Discipline that is based on moral persuasion involves discussion, praise for correct behavior, negotiation, and parental modeling of good behavior. In schools, democratic discipline involves teaching methods that emphasize cooperation, appropriate ways to dissent, and respect for the rights of others. In a democracy schools should be exemplars of due process and reflect principles of participatory democracy.

So where do you stand in relation to the two opposing views of authoritarian versus democratic discipline? Do you believe that kids are basically good? Are you willing to use rational persuasion, positive reinforcement, and limited punishment, knowing this will take more time and you won't always get immediate compliance? Or do you see kids as basically bent on selfish, uncontrolled behavior? Do you expect immediate compliance that can be obtained by punishment, especially when the punishment involves the use of pain?

Of course, most parents are somewhere in between the two ends of the continuum. It doesn't mean that you are a full-fledged fascist if you hit your kids, nor does it mean that you are Mahatma Ghandi if you never punish children in any way. Later in this book we will more extensively discuss the middle ground that distinguishes effective discipline.

Since we have begun to talk about punishment, it is a good idea to define what we mean by this term.

Punishment

Punishment has many meanings for many people. However, let's start with a scientific definition. *Punishment is an event or stimulus that decreases the behavior preceding it*. For instance, if admonishing a child once for cursing stops that behavior, you may assume that the admonishment was a punishment. However, if your admonishment does not decrease the cursing, it was not a punishment.

If what you do to stop misbehavior does not stop it, it is not a punishment, although it may satisfy the popular definition of punishment just by causing suffering, pain, or loss. For example, consider school suspension, the standard penalty facing children who misbehave because they hate school. The more children hate school the more they want to cut school. But what happens when they cut school? The authorities tell them they will be suspended and won't be able to come back for a specified number of days. Big deal!

So what happens the next time they cut school? You got it. They get suspended. Great, now they can spend even more time watching TV, doing nothing, getting into trouble, and avoiding schoolwork. Call this a punishment? Is anyone home here?

Punishment as it is generally used is very appealing because it can produce very quick short-term results. It doesn't take much thinking, it usually costs nothing, and most parents and teachers feel they don't need to be trained in its use. But effective punishment is not as simple as some people think. To succeed, it must be carefully tailored both to the recipient and to the behavior in question, something difficult to achieve by instinct or accident. There are some scientific guidelines based on extensive research, but the information is not widely available—and even at its best, the problem with attempted punishment remains that it is the least effective way to stop misbehavior. If it doesn't work immediately, the punisher must increase the frequency, duration, and intensity of the punishment until it finally works. That is one reason why spanking, when ineffective, can escalate to severe abuse. Further, when the punisher is not around there is no motivation for the child to behave. For example, most people who are inclined to exceed the speed limit in their cars will not speed if they know there is a policeman around. Although we still need speeding laws and punishments, it is obvious that they haven't stopped all speeders. Yet, while punishment is the least desirable method to control behavior, we still need to use it sometimes.

Corporal Punishment

Dictionary, legal, educational, and psychological definitions of corporal punishment indicate that it consists of the purposeful infliction of pain on the human body as a penalty for an offense. Although spanking at home and paddling at school are the most common types of corporal punishment, legal precedents have broadened the definition, especially when the pain inflicted is excessive. So it also may include painful confinement in a restricted space, forcing a child to assume a fixed posture for a long time, excessive exercise and drills, forced ingestion of noxious substances, and exposure to painful environments. Also, the courts include the concept of intent when dealing with excessive corporal punishment in considering whether the punisher meant to inflict pain.

For instance, the usual legal definition cited here was used by a defendant teacher in litigation against her and the Washington D.C. school board. The plaintiff student had been blowing spit bubbles in the air and the teacher claimed that this disgusting, unsanitary act had caused her to "instinctively" strike out. Her smack on his mouth caused bleeding, pain, and emotional trauma. Her defense was based, in part, on the school board regulations that defined corporal punishment as an "intentional" act. She stated that she hadn't intended to hit the child; therefore, her instinctive act had not violated the school board regulations. Rather than face the plaintiffs in court, the defendants settled the case through attorneys. Following the settlement, the school board also removed the term "intentional" from its definition of corporal punishment.

Inflicters' and inflictees' definitions and perceptions of pain may vary. Therefore, accurate definitions in individual cases are debatable, especially in drawing a line between allowable corporal punishment and abuse. State and local education and human services regulations that allow the use of corporal punishment normally include restrictions meant to ensure that its use is not abusive.

Twenty-seven states forbid corporal punishment in schools. No state forbids parental spanking, but thirty-seven states prohibit foster parents from spanking. Forty-two do not allow corporal punishment in residential institutions and agency group homes, thirty-nine forbid it in day-care centers and thirty-two in family care centers. If parental spanking or other punishment causes bruises or welts, parents may be charged with child abuse. In many states, teachers may legally bruise students.

School paddlers are admonished to use reasonable force, to assure that they are not striking in anger, and to have a witness present. Although written reports are required and parents must normally be notified, data and our personal observations indicate that most school districts sustain some amount of unreported informal corporal punishment.

Smacking and Whacking in Schools—Is This Pedagogy?

Most corporal punishment in schools is administered with wooden paddles. Some schools specify the shape, size and thickness of the paddle and the number of blows per offense.

My students and I have documented incidents of corporal pun-ishment in the national press over a twenty-five-year period. Instru-ments used include leather straps, thin rattan switches, baseball bats, plastic bats, the soles of size 13 cowboy boots, and a variety of other handy or favored instruments. Students have been confined for long periods in storerooms, boxes, cloakrooms, closets, and school vaults. They have been thrown against lockers, walls, desks, or concrete pillars and forced to run a gauntlet or "belt line."

The inventiveness of teachers who inflict pain on children appears to be unlimited. In the late 1980s, I conducted clinical eval-uations of students in the Ennis, Montana, public schools, where children who misbehaved were "racked up." I wasn't sure what racking meant until it was described in detail by one of the students. The process involves teachers grabbing children by the neck and lifting them up enough so that they begin to choke. This process is accompanied by screaming and yelling statements until the child gets the message. Clinical evaluations and the efforts of Eileen White and her husband, local veterinarians, helped arouse the ire of Montana legislators, who finally banned corporal punishment in that state.

The cases reported are relatively rare, however, and when these offenses occur they are often considered necessary, acceptable, and legal in schools and communities where they happen. Yet the dam-age caused by educators often rises to the legal definition of abuse when committed by parents or adults in any other setting.

It is difficult to determine the extent to which schools use cor-poral punishment—the problems of collecting data are obvious. That is, for paddling incidents to appear in data summaries the teacher has to publicly indicate a paddling occurred by making an official report. Next, the principal has to collect the report and send it to the main office of the school district. Finally, the district has to agree to share the information with the public. Even when all this happens, the reports don't include many accounts of spontaneous hits, smacks, and shoves that are inflicted on students when educa-tors lose their tempers.

Teachers, like parents, sometimes lose it and smack kids even when they are not supposed to. For instance, I and other staff members from the NCSCPA conducted a student discipline survey in an urban New Jersey school district. Even though corporal punishment has been banned for over a hundred years in that state, 5 percent of the students said they had been hit at least once by an educator. This despite the fact that New Jersey educators have been suspended and fired for hitting students.

Biannual Office of Civil Rights (OCR) surveys collected the only national data on corporal punishment in schools. Over the years I extrapolated that data, which for many reasons usually underestimated the actual number of paddlings and hitting incidents in public schools. The surveys never included data from private and parochial schools, where we know from informal reports that many students have received corporal punishment.

Although in the past large numbers of Catholic school students were hit, to the surprise of many adults who survived the rulers of demanding nuns, most dioceses no longer endorse the use of corporal punishment. To make up for this lack of religious zeal, the growing number of students who attend fundamentalist Christian schools have picked up the slack. From informal reports and newspaper accounts of abuses, we know that corporal punishment is widely used in these settings.

In the early 1980s, my guesstimates are for about three million incidents of smacking, swatting, and paddling of schoolchildren per year. In the early 1990s, about half a million swats probably occurred. The OCR has stopped analyzing data, so we don't have any figures past 1992.

Guess who gets hit the most? Sex, age, and size definitely make a difference. In schools and in homes, boys get hit much more frequently than girls. Corporal punishment occurs more frequently in the primary and intermediate levels, where the students are still too small to hit back effectively. Also, students who are hit frequently tend to be the ones with behavioral, academic, learning, and motivational problems. Many of them drop out of school as soon as they can.

Among the Western democracies, our peculiar penchant for paddling schoolchildren is shared only with Canada, New Zealand (which restricts caning to preadolescents) and parts of Australia. All other Western democracies and many other countries forbid corporal punishment in schools.

Banning of school corporal punishment in all those countries was done at the national level. So if you are an adherent of local control and shrink at the thought of more federal regulations in America, do not fear. I have testified in Congress on a bill to ban hitting special education students, including those who are blind, deaf, and severely disturbed. It did not touch the treatment of other students. Judging from the reactions of congressmen from North Carolina and Texas, to name a few, you would have thought that this modest proposal was a Communist plot to undermine the sanctity of school authorities and the safety of all students.

In my opinion, even though over half the states now forbid school paddlings, progress has been stopped by a block of rural, conservative, and mostly Southern and Southwestern states. So if you live in the Bible Belt, don't hold your breath waiting for federal laws to protect your children from a beating in school.

Socioeconomic Status and Racial Factors

Most studies of school corporal punishment indicate that lower-class children are hit four to five times more often than middle- and upper-class children. Because it is more likely that children born African American or Hispanic instead of white will be poor, it is difficult to determine whether paddlings are racially motivated. Further, although no data are available, observations suggest that minority teachers may be just as likely to use corporal punishment on poor minority children as are white teachers.

My research and clinical experience indicate that educators rarely paddle children of wealthy or influential families. I don't know of any elite boarding or independent schools that allow the use of corporal punishment. All the cases of severe paddlings with which I am familiar involve children of poor, blue-collar, or middle-class

parents. There is no question about these data about school paddlings, but the issue of social class and racial predictors of parental
spanking is quite controversial.

Early research on social class and corporal punishment was
inconclusive, although the consensus appeared to favor the belief
that higher socioeconomic status (SES) parents were less likely to
hit their children than were lower SES parents. Some contemporary research continues to suggest that parents in higher SES groups
are less likely to use or approve hitting children as a means of discipline. However, artifacts including the types of questions asked and
who is asking them may bias responses.

Although SES is important, educational level may be more crucial in how survey respondents answer questions about corporal
punishment. Perhaps financial resources or occupational experiences are not as important as educational attainment in determining how people view the act of hitting a child. Education can shape
attitudes and beliefs and can expose people to thinking that con-
tradicts traditional beliefs or transgenerational values regarding
discipline. Further, respondents from higher SES may be more sophisticated about surveys and more likely to respond in terms of the
perceived social desirability of their answers. That is, even if they
do hit their children, they might deny it when asked.

Children with Disabilities

Exceptional children are particularly vulnerable (both physically
and emotionally) because their misbehaviors are often directly related to their disabilities. From an early age, children with Attention-
Deficit Hyperactivity Disorder, learning disabilities, and emotional
problems act in ways that often anger their parents. Even before
they get to school many of these children have been spanked extensively. Then they get paddled in school for behaviors that are often
the result of frequently being hit at home. That is, the more these
children express their anger and frustration by noncompliant
behaviors at home, the more they get hit. The more they get hit,

the angrier they get. The angrier they get, the more aggressive they become. And so it goes in a vicious cycle.

While you might understand how teachers could become easily frustrated with aggressive, disturbed students who are constantly oppositional and defiant, you can be assured that paddling is based on equal opportunities for all children with disabilities.

For example, in one of the many cases in our files at the NCSCPA, an arthritic and rheumatic 3rd-grade boy was spanked with a wooden drawer divider, even after the mother indicated that she did not want her child spanked. In another case, a seven-year-old child had an epileptic seizure due to the stress of being spanked. This was her first convulsion in over a year. An asthmatic ten-year-old girl was struck across the chest because she mispronounced a word during reading class, and despite admonitions from physicians and parents, a boy with orthopedic and heart problems was forced into a "gut run." He dropped dead before it was completed.

How Much Do Parents Hit Their Kids?

Whether or not any particular SES group has the claim to being Number One on the hit parade, you don't have to be an anthropologist or study ancient or distant cultures to understand that we have a problem. We don't get it when scholars and child-care workers keep telling us about the relation between our high regard for spanking and our high rates of violence and child abuse as compared with many other contemporary societies.

Now you may agree that laws should stop school authorities from hitting your kids, especially when you specifically tell them not to. After all, educators are not family. They don't love your kid like you do. Besides, you may know that where paddling is legal, educators can severely bruise kids with little fear of prosecution because they are not covered by state child abuse laws. But if your kid is severely bruised and does not want to go back to school, like so many I have worked with, you might well want the feds to step in.

But how do you feel about the feds coming into your home and telling you not to hit your own kid? Isn't this a violation of family values? Don't you have a right to discipline your kid without having to worry about going to jail? Surely, no government in a free society should be allowed to interfere with a parent's inalienable right to give a toddler a love pat on the behind. After all, isn't it ridiculous to make a federal case out of the swat you gave five-year-old Johnny when he tried to shove his three-year-old sister into the toilet? If so, you agree with most Americans.

Currently, allowing for differences in various polls and honesty in responding, I believe that at least 75 percent of American parents rely on spanking as regular disciplinary procedure or as a so-called last resort. Further, at least 90 percent of American parents have spanked each of their kids at least once. Let's take a brief look at the actual research on how often average American kids get hit by parents or teachers.

A Harris poll that I helped conduct in 1982 revealed that 86 percent of Americans approved of parental spankings. A more recent review of many polls found that between 60 percent and 90 percent of all parents surveyed by the various pollsters reported using some form of physical punishment on their children, with the lowest rates reported for parents of adolescents and the highest for those with children ages three to six. So we know that the older you get the less likely you are to be hit. If you are a toddler, you are in trouble. Almost every study shows that over 90 percent of parents report that they have spanked their toddlers. One survey reported a rate of physical punishment of almost 100 percent for children around three years of age.

Part of the problem of collecting really accurate data has to do with whom you ask. Spankers tend to report less spanking than do spankees. Parent-reported rates of hitting, spanking, and slapping have generally been lower than those of high school students and young adults. One study of 679 college students found that over 93 percent had experienced some physical punishment, primarily by parents (88 percent), and secondarily by teachers (22 percent).

In the home, spanking with the hand is the most common practice. One of my students did a study of college students' memories of parental hitting. They were asked to report how they were hit. Because some were hit in many ways, the percentages do not equal 100 percent. Sixty-three percent indicated they had been spanked. Forty-two percent said they were slapped, 20 percent had their hair or ears pulled, 11 percent were whipped (often with a leather belt, electrical cord, or coat hanger), 9 percent had been punched, 9 percent were severely shaken, 8 percent had their arms twisted, 6 percent were kicked, and 4 percent were pinched. These results are similar to those of other studies.

While I don't think anyone really knows the actual rate of spanking, it is obvious, despite problems of collecting accurate information, that most American kids will experience being hit by an adult. But these statistics are really meaningless in terms of how each child feels about and reacts to being hit. The severity of each spank, the number of times the child is struck, and how long a spanking session lasts all vary and have different meanings in each family.

For instance, parents who have grown up in violent homes may consider a few slaps on the behind to be merely love pats. Those love pats may be hard enough to leave bruises, which can be legally interpreted as evidence of child abuse. Parents who themselves have grown up abused may not distinguish between what they call a love pat and others might call a beating.

In summary, there are many social, economic, educational and transgenerational factors that affect the use of corporal punishment and children's perceptions of it. The bottom line for me is that it is done too much, it is generally ineffective, and it is never necessary. What I know about it is invaluable in understanding and helping parents who come to me with discipline problems.

So, Big Deal, I Give My Kids a Few Swats a Week

In my work as a therapist and school consultant in the area of misbehavior, I find that corporal punishment has been used extensively on the majority of oppositional, defiant, misbehaving children I see. When I get the family history and come to the question of paddling or spanking, I always ask teachers or parents the following questions: "Does it work?" and "What do you think is normal for the numbers of times children should be hit?"

Let me share with you a typical case that illustrates this and some other points I have made. (All the names used in the cases throughout this book are pseudonyms.) This case represents a rather simple problem with a simple solution.

The Drs. Brown

The Drs. Brown are very highly educated, focused people. Forty-year-old Dr. June Brown has a Ph.D. in chemistry and is an executive in a corporation. Dr. Ken Brown, forty-three years old, is a physician who works full time on the staff of a major metropolitan hospital. Needless to say, like many contemporary couples, their lives are characterized by constant stress brought on by time pressures associated with their jobs, routine household chores, and the needs of their two children.

The Browns originally came to me for marriage counseling. What precipitated the visits was a recent argument that ended with Ken hitting June. She became scared, and he was quite remorseful and agreed to come to see me.

After twenty minutes of interview, it was obvious that a major problem in their communications was that they disagreed on disciplining their children. Realizing this, the children instinctively played them against each other, and they obliged by constant arguments and inconsistent discipline procedures. These added to their stress and caused problems in other areas of their relationship.

One thing they both did was spank the children. But June felt guilty about it while Ken claimed it was necessary. In fact, he felt that the kids probably didn't get spanked enough. The couple had read about time out and used it extensively last year, but lately it didn't work.

The children were increasingly becoming more difficult to manage at home and at school. They had begun to get complaints about Joe, their seven-year-old son, who refused to cooperate in school when he didn't like assignments or requests from his 2nd-grade teacher. At home Joe often hit his three-year-old sister, Ruth. What really upset the Browns was that Joe was beginning to lie a lot. He lied about homework, hitting his sister, and taking his sister's toys.

Ruth often had temper tantrums, wouldn't eat her food, and was beginning to imitate her brother.

I will not relate the full family history, which took me two hours to compile. Of interest is that both parents had been spanked as kids. But although June was generally well behaved and "only" got spanked about once a month for petty offenses, her recalcitrant older brother was hit weekly.

June's parents were very demanding. Her father, an engineer with a large corporation, was somewhat cold and distant. Her mother, who could be very affectionate at times, often nagged and screamed at June's brother.

Ken's father was a prominent physician who was able to maintain a practice despite his sometimes explosive temper. He was a perfectionist who was hyper-critical of his three children. Ken, the oldest, despite his high intelligence and his good athletic ability and skill, was constantly at war with his father. Ken had a violent temper when he was young, but got it under control by the time he graduated from high school.

Ken's father often came home angry, ranting about the incompetents with whom he had to work. After a few martinis, he could withdraw or become very explosive about some minor misbehavior of one of his children. Ken's mother was an alcoholic. She was nurturing when sober, but when drunk she was withdrawn and sullen.

Here is part of the first interview.

ME: So, to summarize what you have told me so far, your major concern is that your children are out of control. Also, you disagree on what to do with them, but you both generally spank them when they misbehave. Can you tell me how often each of you spanks Joe, who seems to be the biggest problem?

KEN: What do you mean? I guess not too much. I spank him when he deserves it. Not any more than most parents would.

ME: No, I mean on the average how many times do you hit him. Like, is it once a day, once a week, several times a week, several times a month?

KEN: Oh, I guess I hit him three or four times a week.

ME: June, what about you?

JUNE: I guess I give him a little swat about twice a week.

ME: What do you usually hit him for?

JUNE: Well, we can't stand him taking toys away from his sister, hitting her, not picking up his clothes, and refusing to do what we tell him to do.

KEN: What really bothers me is when he stands there, looks me in the eye, and lies. When I catch him doing that I smack him.

ME: Let's take one of those things. How long has he been hitting his sister?

JUNE: He started to really hit her about six months ago.

ME: When did you start spanking him for that?

JUNE: We tried time-out for the about the first month. We would send him to his room for half an hour. But it didn't help, so we started to spank him every time he laid a hand on his sister.

ME: Did he stop the hitting after you spanked him?

JUNE: Yeah. For that day. But then he would hit her in the next day or two.

ME: So spanking didn't stop him.

JUNE: I guess you could say that.

ME: So why do you keep hitting him if it doesn't work?

KEN: What the hell else are we supposed to do?

JUNE: That is why we are here. I have been telling Ken that this isn't working, and he says it worked with him and it should work with the kids. Isn't that what most parents do?

ME: Yes. How often do you think most parents spank kids at this age?

KEN: Oh, I think it is normal to get spanked at least once a week.

ME: I believe that is not normal or effective. After all, in your own words, you are telling me it doesn't really work. But Ken, what was your model for disciplining kids? From what you have told me, and your wife agrees, you were abused. Your father taught you that losing your temper frequently and hitting as a solution to problems are normal behaviors. You said that you hated these traits in your father, but here you are doing the same thing. No one has taught you how to handle your temper and raise kids without hitting them.

JUNE: He is right, Ken. You are becoming like your father, and Joe is also learning to lose his temper. We have to do something about this. The kids are afraid of you, and after you hit me, I am scared. You never hit me before.

KEN: I know, I know. I am becoming what I hated. But that is why I came here.

ME: Ken, I recognize that you want to change. I am going to give you techniques to recognize and control your anger. But I want you both to agree to stop hitting the kids. I am going to set you up with a behavioral program that is based on positive reinforcement before you leave today.

Because the Browns were highly motivated and able to be consistent, they were capable of following my suggestions. Our first session caused Ken to have flashbacks all week about his father. He began to see that he was doing some of the exact same things his father did. He felt even worse and was determined to change. June was relieved to learn how to use other, positive techniques, which she already knew something about. They both read some handouts I gave them and came every week to our appointments.

After fifteen sessions, both parents were pleased that the children had changed dramatically. Ken learned techniques to recognize the triggers that led to losing his temper—the ones I describe in Chapter Seven. We had a few individual sessions to help him better understand what had happened to him as a victim of abuse and how this related to other problems in his life. We did some work on marital communications, especially around the issues of discipline and appropriate expressions of feelings.

These are topics I return to later in the book. First, however, we need to discuss the differences and similarities between discipline, spanking, and abuse.

2

Abuse or Discipline?

I loved my dad, and I still miss him, even though he passed away over twenty years ago. In many ways he epitomized the American Dream. Let me explain.

My paternal grandparents were Russian immigrants who began life in the east side of New York with almost nothing. My grandmother, who spoke little English, became a widow when my father and his brother were quite young. Knowing that she had little chance of making a life for herself or of remarriage as an illiterate widow with small children, she shipped her sons off to live with a succession of relatives. She then recreated herself as an eligible, childless prospective bride.

Through successful networking among her family and their acquaintances in the trade, she identified and snared a young and promising jeweler from Philadelphia. After establishing a business in cooperation with my grandmother's extended and rapidly growing family of jewelers at North Jersey shore resort towns, her husband was ready to begin a family.

At some unrecorded time before she became pregnant, Grandma Molly must have said something like, "Oh, I forgot to tell you that I already have two sons who will be coming to live with us!"

There are no family archives that reveal the specifics of Grandpa Hyman's reaction, but in a variation on the usual theme he became the wicked stepfather. Needless to say, psychological and physical maltreatment were not uncommon to my father, who was forced to leave school after the 5th grade to work in the family business. While his half-siblings all got much higher levels of education—one became a prominent surgeon—my father struck out on his own. He started a jewelry business that consisted mainly of peddling merchandise on the road. Most customers couldn't pay all at once so they paid on time. My father made the rounds to customers' homes each week. After socializing, maybe having a cup of coffee or some other snack and perhaps selling his hosts something new, he usually collected anywhere from 25 cents to $1.

Dad eventually opened a successful store in Belmar, New Jersey, and became a well-known merchant, prominent citizen, and pillar of the local synagogue. As a member and officer of many business and fraternal organizations, he most cherished his role every Christmas. Representing the Kiwanis, at Christmastime each year he donned a Santa Claus costume and was flown in a small plane to present gifts to the poor children in a regional home for children susceptible to tuberculosis.

Most of the time when I think of Dad, who died in 1967, I think of all the odds he had to overcome to provide a comfortable life for his family. Despite the early abuse in his life, he was generally a gentle person who tried his best, without any model from his own childhood, to be a good father. But too often, and way out of proportion to the many positive aspects of his parenting, memories of his belts and leather razor strop pop into my mind.

Now, for most readers younger than I and those who are uninformed, a strop (yes, that is strop, not strap) consists of two pieces of leather fastened together at the top. The rough and smooth leather strops are about four inches wide and two feet long. Strops are designed for sharpening straight razors, but in my father's day they were often considered admirable substitutes for leather belts when applied to the bottoms of errant children. In those days, when a mom said to her child, "Wait until your father gets home," she was not referring to the pleasure of spending quality time with a dad who was happy to be home from a grueling job and a long commute.

Let me share with you one particular strop-related memory that, depending on my frame of mind, evokes feelings of humor, dismay, or incredulity.

For some unremembered offense, while refusing to comply with a request from my father, I must have retorted with a particularly offensive remark. In my early adolescence I seemed to have a singular ability to enrage my father, who was generally known as a good-natured, jovial guy. We were in the kitchen at the time, and my mother, who had reported my offenses of the day to my father, was beginning to regret snitching on me as my dad became more and more enraged. I knew it was time to depart when his escalating angry verbiage was accompanied by the simultaneous removal of his belt.

To this day I clearly remember that pile of laundry on the landing where the steps to the second floor took a turn. Thinking it would slow my father, I leapt over it on my ascent to the hoped-for haven of my bedroom. My father, screaming in anger for me to stop, was not deterred, and in an amazingly deft feat for a middle-aged man with a potbelly, he leapt over the laundry in hot pursuit, only to stop at the bathroom to abandon his belt for the more fearsome razor strop. It is then that I knew that I was in really big trouble.

Somewhere in the background I could hear my mother, trailing behind, yelling at him to calm down. I knew I had to do something drastic to save my behind. Therefore, using all of the dexterity I could muster, I threw open the window of my second-floor bedroom, pushed up the hinged wooden screen, and slid out so that by grasping the windowsill I was able to dangle from the second floor. I felt that my strategy was brilliant. If my mom didn't arrive in time to calm down my father, I could drop to the ground, I hoped without injury, and make my escape until my dad relented. If I broke a leg, I wouldn't have to run because my father would be diverted by my mother's screaming, his own guilt, and the need to take me to the hospital.

My mom's arrival on the scene and my father's incredulity that his son was so afraid that he jumped out of a second-story window probably saved the day. I don't remember much of what followed, but I do remember that I didn't have to drop to the ground and that everyone calmed down.

Fortunately, this incident was my most dramatic and unusual encounter with the strop. But I remember being spanked, slapped, and smacked by hand, belt, and strop at least four or five times a year through early adolescence. Although I would now consider a "spanking" that employs the use of leather implements to be a beating, I have difficulty using the word as applied to the discipline I received from my father. While I would now consider that abuse, it's hard for me to think of my own loving father as an abuser. I still have this vague notion, reinforced by many relatives over the years, that I got what I deserved. In any event, during sentimental moments I think that it couldn't have been that bad, because look how I turned out. I share this unfortunate rationalization, based on what logicians call the *naturalistic fallacy*, with many other Americans. It is unfortunate because it is used to justify everything from mild swats to severe abuse. It is the kind of thinking that is related to our tolerance of a wide range of ills visited upon the lives of children.

The naturalistic fallacy is based on the assumption that because something already exits, it should continue to exist. Just because our parents hit us, we should hit our children.

Growing up in the forties and fifties, I was probably spanked no more than most of my friends and probably much less than those who were known to have fathers who couldn't control their drinking and tempers. Yet over fifty years later, as a psychologist with extensive experience in the area of discipline and child abuse, if I heard a story similar to the one I have related, I would consider it a case of abusive parenting. In fact, I would be required by law to report this incident if I suspected child abuse, even though I observed no bruises.

Changing perceptions of allowable levels of spanking, smacking, whipping, and slapping of American children have caused turmoil among parents, advocates of differing persuasions, and policymakers. At one end of the spectrum are those who claim that any spanking, no matter how light, is child abuse. At the other end are those, often rooted in fundamentalist religious ideology, who scoff at the idea that God would command the use of a practice that was abusive. In between are most of the public, who haven't really thought much about it. They were spanked, they spank or spanked their own children, so for them there is no big deal about this practice that has continued through countless generations. That is, until someone accuses them of abuse or they are really made to think about the issue. But before we discuss this debate in more detail and I tell you my opinion, let's define abuse.

Defining Child Abuse

Every state legally defines child abuse and neglect. Generally, physical child abuse occurs when caretakers or others inflict physical injury by hitting, punching, beating, kicking, throwing, biting, burning, or otherwise physically harming a child. Proof is usually determined by the presence of welts, marks, minor to major bruises, abrasions, lacerations, eye injuries, fractures, and damage to internal organs. Laws also cover extreme or bizarre forms of punishment such as torture or confinement in dark closets, boxes, or rooms for days or longer periods.

It wasn't until the publication of a book called *The Battered Child* (edited by two doctors, Ray Helfer and C. Henry Kempe) in 1969 that the public and professionals began to think seriously of the medical, social, and ethical ramifications of allowing parents to beat their children. The next significant milestone occurred in 1974, when the president signed into law the Child Abuse and Prevention Treatment Act.

Some Facts About Abuse

Currently, every state has some form of child abuse law, supported by a bureaucracy to deal with identification, diagnosis, treatment, and prevention. One of the significant aspects of these state laws is mandatory reporting of sexual, emotional, and physical abuse and neglect. This mandate applies to all citizens alike and even breaches the sanctity of confidentiality between patient and therapist.

Despite mandatory reporting laws, most of us have on at least one occasion observed a public spanking capable of leaving bruises, and we did nothing. If we spend much time in malls, supermarkets, or traveling, it is not unlikely that we will witness such an event. Tired, cranky, or restless toddlers in tow by tired, cranky, restless parents are at risk of public spankings. Yet rarely do we say something to the parent, let alone report the incident.

When observing a temper tantrum by a parent, I bet that on at least one occasion you have thought to yourself something like, "If that kid gets walloped that badly in public, I wonder what happens at home where no one can see," or "I should probably do something or intervene but it is none of my business." After all, there is no law saying parents can't hit their own kids whenever and wherever they wish. Why make a federal case of an overzealous spanking?

I have often been appalled by public parental temper tantrums, but like most of us, I have been reluctant to intervene. However, a social worker in Texas told me about her technique. When she sees a frustrated, angry parent slapping a child around, she approaches the parent and says, "You must really be frustrated, it is so hard to make children behave in public. I really know how you feel. Is there anything I can do to help you?" This approach helps the angry parent to recognize that others are sympathetic to the difficulties of managing children in public while trying to shop or accomplish other chores. The parent is not accused of abuse or given other messages about being inadequate. You might want to try this technique or some variation and see what happens.

Child abuse is widely recognized and publicized in our country. Probably every day at least one newspaper in this country reports a particularly brutal case of child abuse, often ending in death for the child. National child protection and advocacy groups periodically issue reports about our horrendous rates of abuse. We really don't know the exact rates of child abuse, but we do know they are too high. For instance, the National Center on Child Abuse and Neglect figures from 1993 were 200,000 reported cases of abuse. But in 1995, a study done by the Gallup Organization estimated the actual incidence to be around 3 million. Interestingly, these data are based on parents' own reports rather than official government documents. We could even probably up the numbers based on the research of Anthony Graziano, a prominent corporal punishment researcher. All of his data indicate that when asked about hitting (not necessarily abuse as legally defined), children always report more hitting than their parents do.

All studies indicate that boys are hit much more frequently than girls. Many surely learn that hitting is a way to solve problems, or at least that it is an acceptable manner of venting frustrations. A poll of young people found that 40 percent of girls aged fourteen to seventeen reported that they knew at least one peer who had been hit or beaten by a boyfriend. To me and many other behavioral scientists, the connection between parental spanking and girlfriend hitting is pretty clear.

Child abuse, at least in the abstract, is widely recognized in our society. Talk shows, especially those such as *Oprah* and *Geraldo*, regularly feature guests who address the issue. Numbers for state child abuse hot lines are well publicized and easily obtainable. There have been enough movies and TV shows about abuse that it may be pretty graphic in the minds of many.

Diagnosis of physical child abuse is made by professionals. Most frequently, when physical manifestations occur, medical authorities examine the child. However, most psychologists, social workers, and other mental health professionals who work with children are also trained to identify abuse. Significantly, the emotional symptoms of any type of abuse are the most devastating and long lasting. So, how can what I have described be connected to "normal" spanking? Let me use a school problem to illustrate my point.

If you are like the majority of Americans, you probably see no harm in a loving pat on your child's behind, as long as it is not too hard. But what is too hard? You might answer that you, as a loving parent, know what is too hard. But how would you feel about a teacher or principal who applied a three-quarter-inch wooden paddle to little Jimmy's derriere, and despite bruises didn't feel that the paddling was too hard? Finally, could you control yourself if the principal informed you, "Whether you like it or not, Jimmy will be paddled when he deserves it"?

Even though as a parent you don't want your kid paddled by a stranger, you may have no choice. Many states give schools the same rights that you have as a parent to discipline your child—and each paddler determines how hard to hit each child. Since states don't forbid spanking by parents, in states where school corporal punishment is legal, educators may also spank. This is because of a legal precedent based on the old English tradition and law of "in loco parentis," and there isn't much you can do about it. Yet that means your concept of the difference between a spanking and abuse may be quite different from the concept of a paddling principal.

All studies of attitudes about spanking and paddling show that the greatest support is in conservative and rural regions of the country. This is especially true in the South, where the majority of reported school paddlings take place. If you lived in the South, or even in rural areas of states like Pennsylvania or Delaware, how would you feel if your child was paddled so severely that an examining physician filed child abuse charges—only to discover that the beating was legal because it was defined as a form of school discipline protected by state law? You would then learn that children in public schools are the only people in America who have no constitutional protection from beatings by authorities. In fact, you might feel quite like any parent of a schoolchild in a pro-corporal-punishment state.

Death by Discipline

Most parents who punish their children to death claim that they didn't mean to kill them. Few think of hands as deadly weapons, but in a way, a severe spanking might be analogous to an accidental

shooting. There are many cases where children get shot accidentally because guns were available. Hitting the kids is an available
procedure for parents, and there are cases where it "accidentally"
leads to death, too.

Of course I have heard the argument that it is not guns that kill
people, it is people who kill people. But if you accept this reasoning,
shouldn't it apply to spanking? It is not their hands, fists, electrical
cords, whips, or other instruments that kill the children, it's the parents who do it. Sounds somewhat silly to me. But as is demonstrated
in many other countries such as Japan and Singapore, it is possible
to limit gun ownership and therefore reduce death by guns. In the
same vein you could eliminate severe spankings by eliminating the
acceptance of spanking. If no child were spanked, none would be
spanked severely, thereby reducing deaths of children in their
homes. But let us return to reality.

A person who shoots someone out of anger or fear could claim
to have meant only to scare, stop, or wound the victim. This seems
like a stretch to make a point. However, both spanking and shooting inflict pain. In both cases the purpose is to punish or deter someone from a specific behavior. In fact, threatening with a gun should
have the same type of deterrence value as threatening with a spanking. That is, both convey to potential victims that if they don't
behave in a certain way they will receive pain. The less they comply,
the more the potential for pain and harm. This is the type of thinking that occurs when some parents beat their children to death.

Several years ago, Greg Roper (a graduate student in school psychology) and I decided to determine how often children died as the
result of severe corporal punishment and in the name of discipline.
Because the information we wanted was difficult to obtain from
official records of abuse agencies and police departments, we conducted a national search using newspaper accounts. From 300 newspaper accounts of caretakers charged with the murder of children,
we were able to study 201 cases in which the articles provided
enough information for our study.

In the 201 identified cases, 41 percent of the caretakers stated
that the deaths occurred because they were trying to discipline the

children. In 31 percent of the identified cases, the caretakers merely indicated that deaths occurred as a result of punishment procedures, but gave no real reason why the children were being punished to death. Out of the 201 cases one-third of the punishments were clearly severe forms of corporal punishment.

What were the horrendous misbehaviors that ended in death? Some toddlers soiled or wet themselves after many warnings and previous spankings for behavior that was so inconvenient to the caretakers. Some caretakers claimed that the children were "out of control," and others said that the children just "wouldn't behave." Some other misbehaviors that carried the death penalty included stealing, "blocking my view of the TV," and refusal to take out the trash. One victim ate an unauthorized piece of cake; another "wouldn't eat her dinner." One caretaker, explaining why the child was murdered, was quoted as saying, "she was annoying me."

Of course, the above cases are extreme, and the papers may have overstated the circumstances for dramatic effect. But the children are dead. We should return to a question I asked earlier. Would these cases have occurred if Americans just didn't think it was ever appropriate to hit children? You may answer that even if we passed laws it wouldn't stop such incidents because there are always people who will defy laws and norms. Also, there will always be some parents who are so mentally deranged that they don't know what they are doing. You are right, but these account for a small percentage of those charged with abuse. In fact, attempts to identify a specific pathological, abusive personality disorder have never been successful. Therefore, it appears that most abusers are "normal" parents who spank, swat, slap, or shake their children overzealously. But what happens when there are laws against spanking?

No Spanking Allowed

As incredible as it might seem to most Americans, spanking in Sweden and some other countries can become a federal case. Other nonspanking countries include Finland, Denmark, Norway, Austria, and Cyprus. In May 1996, the highest court of Italy ruled that parents could no longer hit their children. The court ruled in favor of a ten-year-old girl whose father beat her to "teach her right from wrong." The court implied that the only ones wrong were the father and all other parents who hit children in a "culturally anachronistic" practice.

In Sweden, where corporal punishment was banned in 1979, assessments made in 1981 and in 1988 indicated dramatic reductions in the use of physical punishment, parental commitment to its use, and numbers of cases of child abuse. Instead of arguing with parents whether or not spanking is abuse, professionals have focused their energies on teaching parents to prevent misbehavior and how to deal effectively with it when it does occur.

Most critics of national laws against spanking will probably cite the Scandinavian countries as too permissive and therefore a poor example for disciplining children. But Austria and Italy do not generally fall into that class. Also, how about the fact that since 1992, Germany has been considering abolishment, or that Scotland, Canada, and Bolivia have also been considering similar legislation? So if you lived a country where spanking is forbidden, it is unlikely that you would ever have to question whether you were witnessing a mere spanking or physical abuse. You would recognize that hitting is a type of assault, whether it is an adult inflicting pain on another adult or on a child. You would say that corporal punishment is abuse. The point is, some countries have not chosen to develop elaborate criteria for separating abuse from spanking; it is all the same. But let us turn to the American context and address the question implied in the title of this chapter. Is spanking child abuse?

Spanking on the Continuum of Abuse

There are three distinct views regarding whether spanking is child abuse. It isn't abuse, it is abuse, or it is sub-abusive.

Spanking Is Not Abuse

Traditionalists would argue that spanking has always been a part of parenting. They point to the fact that most of us have been spanked and we survived quite well. They are against abuse, but they also feel that government should not dictate family values and methods of discipline. Some think that most child abuse legislation is too intrusive to the family, and they therefore constantly attempt to weaken the authority of the child abuse agencies.

The growing, markedly right-wing resistance to strong child abuse legislation is claimed to be justified by alleged excesses of police intervention in normal parental discipline. Policy wonks from the political and religious far right illustrate their arguments with cases in which parents have slapped or spanked their kids in public places and then been taken away in handcuffs to be charged and arrested as abusers. They cite reports of children warning parents that if their parents spank them, they will report them to the child abuse hot line. They use Biblical arguments to defend the sanctity of parental authority over intrusion by the state. Further, they object to lack of due process rights when the courts, based on the opinions of social workers or police, summarily remove allegedly at-risk children from homes that officials assert to be life threatening to the children.

Conservative researchers and professionals, whom we will discuss later, claim that "moderate" spanking does no harm and that there is no research to support abolition of this type of spanking, especially with children below five or six years of age.

Spanking Is Abuse

Antispanking advocates tend to be liberal, although some politically conservative theoreticians are against paddling in schools if it is against parental wishes. These include Pat Buchanan, who agreed with me on a radio show. Most well-known child abuse experts and policymakers consider corporal punishment to be abuse. They point out that even though almost everybody agrees that no adult has the right to beat a child to death or to injure children, there is no clear line of demarcation between spanking and abuse. They use the schools as an example of this problem.

Texas allows the use of corporal punishment "up to the point of deadly force." Florida courts say that if a student's bruises from being paddled disappear by the fifth or sixth day after the event, it is not abuse. How far does one go before a paddling is short of deadly force? Why are teachers allowed to bruise children in Florida and parents not? Can the teacher-inflicted bruises be one inch wide, two inches wide, or multiple and four inches wide?

So in Florida schools it may not be so easy to recognize child abuse at the extreme end of the syndrome. In hospitals it is relatively easy. Victims have numerous welts, bruises, and fractures. However, despite the attempts by legislatures, professionals, and the courts to define the line between "normal" punishment and abuse, there is a growing unease and increasing debate about the issue. The solution would be to forbid any hitting of children, just as we do for adults. After all, no one complains that we should not have assault and battery charges for attacks on adults encoded in law.

Despite claims by conservatives that the functionaries who work for child abuse bureaucracies are overly intrusive and too quick to remove children from families, liberals see a different picture. Anti–corporal punishment advocates, many representing a politically liberal consensus, claim that the abuse laws are not effectively enforced to protect children. They point to the lack of appropriate resources, the lack of adequately trained professionals on the front lines, and the high turnover rates of burned out social workers. In almost every state or county setting, child abuse professionals are overloaded with cases and lack adequate facilities to place at-risk children. There are almost daily media accounts of parents who batter and kill their children, despite the fact that they were known as abusers by child welfare officials. Liberals claim that is better to err on the side of children's rights and thereby save lives than to give primacy to parental claims and rights. Too often, in the name of family preservation, at-risk children who had been removed from abusive parents have been returned and later killed.

This position considers hitting within its broader context. Child abuse results from hitting kids very hard. Most abusers, even those who kill their children, as we have shown, frequently state that they acted in the name of discipline. Almost all abuse results from an extreme form of corporal punishment, a disciplinary practice that is widely approved and accepted as necessary.

The exact line where a spank becomes abuse is determined by both subjective and objective criteria. We will never be able to legislate exactly where that line is. There is a wide middle ground that is very much subject to debate. So what is the solution?

Spanking Is Sub-Abusive

The key to understanding whether or not spanking is abuse lies in understanding the intent of the act. Let's face it. When you spank your children, they feel both physical and emotional pain. If truth be known, setting aside all of the rationalizations such as "this hurts me more than you" and "you will thank me some day for teaching you to behave," your intent is to cause discomfort. Therefore, I believe that the intent of spanking is to inflict pain, shock, or fear.

Even with my strong antispanking beliefs, I can't say that a few light smacks on the behind of a two-year-old constitute abuse. But I believe that the crucible of child abuse is that belief that it is all right to use discipline based on the intent to inflict a degree of pain, any degree of pain. While it may be below the point of abuse on a continuum of pain infliction, and subsequently sub-abusive, it is still on that continuum. I believe that Anthony Graziano, who has investigated the process of spanking, first labeled it as sub-abusive violence to resolve the dilemma. This description is supported in Jeff Kaplan's national survey of psychologists, which revealed that 55 percent believe spanking is an abusive act. Because we know that whenever any group is given the power to inflict pain on others that power will inevitably be misused, why are we even debating the issue?

If, as a society, we didn't believe in hitting children at all, would we be concerned about where that line marking abuse is for each child? If all potential parents received training in the many effective preventive and positive approaches to discipline, would there be a debate about a technique that does not have to be used? After all, many families in our society and those in many other countries and cultures educate and parent children without paddles and spanking. If we just didn't spank kids, abuse would be minimal and considered a shocking aberration of the public norms for treating children. But change is difficult.

The problem is that our views about children harbor real paradoxes. The few examples cited suggest that child advocates have had to struggle hard but have been successful in raising the public's consciousness about emerging concepts of threats to children's physical and emotional health. We are now on the threshold of dealing with the idea that hitting itself may be abuse. But there is significant resistance to this idea. The public opposition to change is in part related to religious views about parental rights to spank.

The belief that God commands the use of the rod is a frequent justification of any corporal punishment ranging from a single light spank to undeniable child abuse. We frequently read about cases of abuse in the name of God as interpreted by the leaders of fundamentalist cults. The exploitation of children by David Koresh that ended in the disaster at Waco and the largely forgotten case of Jim Jones in South America are good examples of how the Bible can be used to justify all types of abuse of children. In all of these cases severe physical punishment of children was well ritualized and frequently used. When religion is used as a rationale, it is difficult to convince Americans that public policy that supports swatting, slapping, and smacking children is policy that favors abuse. After all, even in the Bible, Abraham was willing to kill his child as God had ordered. To some, this suggests that fathers can do what they wish with their children.

The fear of change is in part related to our perceptions of ourselves as a nation. If spanking is abuse, would that mean that most Americans when they hit their children are abusers? Wouldn't this include most parents (like my father), many teachers, and the pediatricians who recommend spanking? Yet many people survive spankings and even abuse to become productive citizens, able to laugh about severe spanking, even their own.

For instance, did you get a chance to laugh while watching Bill Cosby on TV or while reading his book in which he describes how he dealt with one of his son's problems? Bill Cosby, the ideal TV dad, humorously recounted using a stick in the family barn to teach his real-life son to never again tell a fib. The audience thought it particularly hilarious when, after several swats, Cosby told his son he wouldn't hit him again. After turning around to leave, he surprised his son with a final hit, thereby demonstrating what it feels like when someone lies.

No one asked why the boy felt he needed to lie, but it certainly was an amusing anecdote for the audience. No one suggested that hitting a kid with a stick falls within the purview of legally defined abuse. But then, Cosby and his audience are not the only ones who think there is something funny about hitting kids.

Did you ever notice how many cartoons about mischievous children feature some type of physical punishment? Despite the fact that spanking, swatting, and hitting are meant to inflict pain, our culture sometimes treats these incidents as jolly fun! But not everyone sees the infliction of pain as funny, and there have always been those who view it as abuse.

Various types of child abuse have been recognized by advocates and writers for many generations. Through literature, many writers have tried to sensitize a reluctant public to act to improve the lot of children. But even today the public is often slow to act. Despite complaints by the religious and political right, historically— and even in contemporary times—the scales have tilted in the direction of traditions, past policies, parental rights, and minimal protection for children. It is difficult to engage politicians, policymakers, and many professionals regarding the relation between spanking and abuse at a time when children appear at risk from many more dire threats. I am not saying that we are totally devoid of concern for children, but there is a trend to procrastinate in the face of need.

For instance, Charles Dickens in *Nicholas Nickleby* described a world of childhood in which dirt and disorder caused much disease. Through significant public consciousness raising, we have progressed to a point where modern hygiene has reduced filth and the spread of many infectious diseases. Yet chemicals in the environment currently affect the lives of too many children—who are substantially more sensitive than adults to the toxic effects of many pollutants. Look at the ongoing struggle to merely maintain—much less improve—laws to guarantee clean air and water. Another example of our reluctance to quickly move public policy is the evidence that many childhood cancers are related to environmental pollutants. These formerly rare conditions now appear at rates of more than six thousand per year, and yet funding for research on the effects of environmental pollutants on the young was at one point discontinued.

Admittedly, sometimes passage of child advocacy legislation backfires. For example, child labor laws, while well meaning, set the stage for another type of abuse by disenfranchising children as economic assets for families. Most Americans, at some level, view children as economic liabilities. The American business establishment exacerbates the problem through manipulation of the kiddie and youth market. Television provides a perfect medium for catching young children and turning them into uncritical consumers. Television executives contribute to what some would consider psychological abuse as they continue to program excessive amounts of violence. The passive acceptance of violence adds to a climate where children readily accept the use of force to solve problems. This includes the acceptance of hitting to solve problems.

In summary, there are three positions regarding how to categorize spanking. Many child abuse workers, experts in discipline, and others consider any spanking to be an act of violence and therefore the result is considered abuse. In opposition, many parents, leaders of the religious right, and conservative politicians distinguish between "normal" spanking and abuse. However, I believe the third position, that spanking is sub-abusive. Because spanking is used to

inflict pain, and because the use of physical pain is neither necessary nor effective in raising and educating children, it should be
considered as an inherently abusive act. The belief that hitting is
OK has caused too much mischief, grief, and even death among
American children.

There is plenty of evidence that children can be raised and educated without spanking them. So why do we do it? I answer that
question in the next chapter.

3

Why We Hit and What It Does to Kids

During family therapy, Jake grew increasingly agitated as we discussed why he did not come home Saturday night, despite his parents' admonitions about his defiance. He provocatively lay there on the couch, his feet on the arm so that the soles of the shoes were partially facing his father, who was seated on another couch. He told his parents that he didn't care what they said. Taking advantage of the freedom to express emotions that all parties agree to in my family therapy sessions, Jake pushed the envelope, "Mom, you can't tell me what to do. All you do is punish me, you bitch."

Jake's father's face began to get red, "You stop talking that way to your mother!"

Jake responded, "Fuck you. Dr. Hyman said we can say anything we want in here. If I want to call Mom a fucking bitch, I will!"

I sat there astounded as an enraged Mr. Grant jumped up from his seat, bounded the three feet to the couch where Jake was reclining and started to punch Jake in the face and head. How could a man with a master's degree, an upper-middle-class corporate executive, a man generally devoted to rational decision making, come to this point in his life? These were some of the thoughts that raced through my mind as I felt the adrenaline coursing through my body telling me, "Do something, do something!"

Mrs. Grant looked toward me in alarm and saw what appeared to be a calm, detached professional. However, my stomach was beginning to churn as my thinking went into high gear, and I swiftly considered my options. My muscles tensed in anticipation of immediate use as I repeatedly but calmly begged and then ordered Mr. Grant to stop hitting his son.

After what seemed an eternity, but in actuality was probably ten to fifteen seconds, Mr. Grant moved backward toward his seat on his couch, which formed a corner with his son's couch. As he did this, Jake followed him up. Jake's arms had been protectively covering his face and head, but as Mr. Grant stopped swinging, Jake retaliated by attempting to punch his father. It was to little avail, since the bigger and stronger Mr. Grant, as he fell back from the onslaught onto his couch, engaged his son in a headlock.

At this point, I told Jake to stop swinging at his father and urged his father to let him go. Neither relented, so—somewhat relieved to expend my increasing supply of adrenaline—I swung into action. I grabbed Jake from behind, I told him I was taking him to the floor and assured him in a calm voice that I would not hurt him. I grabbed his arms, crossed them in front of him in what is called a basket hold and took him to the floor. Using this procedure of therapeutic restraint, I secured him under me with my legs locked around his so he couldn't kick me if he tried.

Jake, with whom I had good rapport, quieted down and started to cry, "You see, you see, that's how my father treats me."

When everyone calmed down and went back to their seats, I said to Mr. Grant, "See how he triggered your anger. You could really have hurt Jake."

He responded, "Are you kidding? If I really wanted to hurt him I would! But I am not going to let him sit there and use that kind of language to me and his mother."

Parents and children frequently tell therapists about the spanking, swatting, and punching that occurs behind the closed doors of their homes, but the actual thrashing of an adolescent by his father during a family therapy session is a truly rare sight. So why I am telling you about this very unusual case? It illustrates how patterns of child rearing can turn into disasters, even though in themselves they do not appear unusual or abusive.

Transgenerational Patterns of Child Rearing

I promised you at the beginning that I would not burden you with a lot of psychobabble. However, to understand discipline, you must understand how *transgenerational patterns of child rearing* bear on the topic. Simply stated, this term refers to family factors that are transmitted from generation to generation. These include personality characteristics such as impulse control, patience, and expressions of emotion, beliefs that shape life views such as religious orientation and regard for education, and specific techniques of child rearing such as those employed in discipline. Let's see how such factors affected what happened to Jake.

First, let me assure you that Mr. Grant is not a monster. When Jake, the oldest of his three children, was born, he could not possibly have envisioned this sad scenario. Although his fourteen-year-old daughter and ten-year-old son have had some problems, neither has aroused him to such intense anger as has Jake. So how could it happen that this successful corporate executive, a man respected in the community and in his church, could be driven to such behavior? Let me share a little background with you.

Mr. and Mrs. Grant, both college educated, brought their son Jake to me because of failing grades, oppositional behavior, temper tantrums, bullying of younger neighborhood children, stealing, lying, and suspected substance abuse. In other words, my kind of kid—or at least the kind of kid that I have worked with for thirty years. During the initial session I interviewed Jake and his parents together, confirmed that the referral problem was accurate, and took a family history.

When Jake was a preschool child, he could be very loving and cute. He seemed quite bright, but at an early age he began to have chronic ear infections that probably contributed to his late development of speech. In day school the teachers noted that he appeared impulsive, sometimes had trouble sharing, and had a very short attention span.

When his sister was born, Jake was about two and a half. His sister had some early medical problems that required a lot of attention.

Jake began demanding attention and often had temper tantrums. On several occasions, he hit the infant and frequently tried to take her toys. The pattern continued as he got older.

During the primary grades, despite the fact that Jake appeared bright, he had trouble learning to read. As homework assignments increased, he frequently tried every avoidance technique known to childhood. His parents took turns in the evening making him sit down and do his work. Tempers often flared from all parties. Jake claimed he couldn't do some of the work but seemed unwilling to concentrate enough for proper learning.

After several years of teacher reports that Jake could do the work if he tried, and constant admonitions at home regarding his laziness and disrespect, he was finally referred to the school psychologist when he was in the 3rd grade. Jake was diagnosed as having Attention-Deficit Hyperactivity Disorder, a mild learning disability related to auditory perception, and Oppositional Defiant Disorder.

Jake was a vulnerable child from the get-go. Because he was bright and was able to compensate to some extent for his learning problem, the problem was not quickly identified. Further, his lack of impulse control and attention were attributed to his being "all boy." His pediatrician and early teachers predicted that he would grow out of his problems as he matured. Because he wasn't diagnosed early enough, his misbehavior bothered his parents to the point that the "normal" amount of spanking began to escalate. Spanking was often accompanied by anger and verbally demeaning comments.

Nobody recognized that Jake's apparent lazy, oppositional, and defiant behaviors occurred because he had real problems focusing, concentrating, and sometimes correctly interpreting what adults were telling him. The birth of his sister signaled to him abandonment by his parents. This was to be expected, but with his problems, he never did make a smooth transition of adjusting to a new sibling.

By 3rd grade, Jake's life was governed by a cycle of misbehavior, punishment, repentance—and the next misbehavior. Guess what the major punishment was? You got it, spanking. Here is how the all-too-familiar scenario went as I interviewed Jake's parents and probed for transgenerational patterns.

ME: So, one of your complaints is that Jake doesn't want to follow any rules. When he is frustrated he loses his temper, curses, screams, and may even throw things around.

MR. GRANT: That's right.

ME: Has he physically threatened either of you?

MRS. GRANT: No—he says that we hate him and he hates us, but he hasn't threatened either of us.

MR. GRANT: That's all he has to do. But he does get wacko when he has these tantrums if he doesn't get his way.

ME: How long has he had this problem with his temper?

MRS. GRANT: Well, I know he had normal temper tantrums when he was two, but they seemed to get worse after his sister was born. We expected some sibling rivalry, and we tried to prepare him for his sister. Of course, we didn't know she would require so much attention.

ME: What did you do when he had tantrums?

MRS. GRANT: Well, I read that you are supposed to ignore them, so I did.

ME: Did that work?

MRS. GRANT: It did for a few months, but then when I ignored him he started going after his sister. Then I started using time-out and spanking. They also worked for while. But he really started to get worse when he was about eight years old.

ME: So what did you do when he lost his temper?

MRS. GRANT: We threatened and carried out all types of punishments. When he used foul language he always got at least one whack. We just won't tolerate that type of language in our home. But we are now at the point where he defies us to punish him. No punishment seems to work.

ME: It sounds to me like you are in a real power struggle, since there is no punishment you can use to control him.

MR. GRANT: You got it. That is why we are here. We are losing control.

ME: Well, it is clear that you need to change your strategy for working with him. This leads to some questions that I always ask in this type of situation. First, which of you has a temper problem?

MR. GRANT: Well, I guess I do. But I try to control it—but Jake really pushes every button on me. He knows just how to get me going.

ME: Mr. Grant, which of your parents had a temper problem?

MR. GRANT: My father did. We never knew when he would blow up. But, of course, he had a hard life growing up with an alcoholic father.

ME: How often were you spanked as you were growing up?

MR. GRANT: I got it on a steady basis until I was about seventeen. At that point I was pretty big. I was bigger than Dad. One day he punched me. I felt it was completely unjustified. I picked up a piece of wood, and I told him that if he ever hit me again I would beat the shit out of him. He was shocked when I raised that two-by-four, and that was the last time he ever hit me.

Learning to Lose Your Temper

This scenario, with minor variations, is so often repeated in my practice that I could substitute the names and some of the details and use it as an account of almost all interviews with families with an impulsive or aggressive child. The point is that unless parents are born with some type of brain dysfunction that causes them to be violent, they learn to lose their tempers from their own parents. The psychologists' term for this is *modeling*—and that's not psychobabble; it's shorthand for a useful insight into how our personalities and behaviors develop.

When parents complain about their child's temper, I invariably discover that at least one parent has a temper problem and at least one of his or her parents had a similar problem. Of course, the same goes for spanking. Now, this does not mean that every child who has a parent with poor impulse control will model this behavior for the next generation. But more often than not, I find that parents who lose their tempers have children who lose their tempers. I feel it is very important to help parents learn this connection, since many think that their own tempers or the tempers of their children are inherited traits. As adults, they often learn to control themselves in most settings, such as at work or in social gatherings. It is ironic that they often accept that they have tempers themselves but are infuriated about this trait in their child.

Many parents of this type do not realize that they are modeling poor impulse control. That is, they are teaching their child by example how to handle frustration badly. The child learns that losing one's temper and hitting are ways to solve problems. If things really escalate, parents literally try to beat the temper out of their child, just as their parents tried to beat it out of them. Obviously, in the case of Jake, the father was doing the more severe spanking, but what about the mother?

ME: Mrs. Grant, how often were you spanked as a child?

MRS. GRANT: Well, I was a good child and the apple of my father's eye. I was his little girl, so I rarely got spanked by him. But he did spank my brother.

ME: How often?

MRS. GRANT: Oh, about two or three times a month until he was in high school. My father was very religious and believed in that old saying about sparing the rod.

ME: OK. Now, how often do each of you spank Jake?

MRS. GRANT: In the last few years I haven't spanked him much. Mostly I scream and yell and threaten him. It doesn't do much good.

MR. GRANT: I don't hit him that much anymore. Maybe once every week or two when he really gets to me with his lying, stealing, and abusing his sister.

ME: And when he was younger?

MR. GRANT: I really got mad about him hitting his sister or teasing her. I generally spanked him several times a week. But it generally wasn't real hard. After all, we didn't abuse him.

MRS. GRANT: Yes, we know better than that. It was usually a few smacks on the behind or on the wrist.

This gives you the flavor of a typical initial interview with the parents of adolescents like Jake. The complete history is too extensive to present here. In summary, after Jake was diagnosed, he was given special help in reading. However, much damage to his self-esteem had been done. He had little trust in adults. His father had modeled violence (hitting) as a solution to his problems. The minor behavioral problems in the primary grades increased after around 6th grade, when he began to hang out with other "troublemakers." His parents tried to restrict association with these undesirable peers, but the more they punished Jake, the more he rebelled. At thirteen he began to dress like a "druggie skater." He wore only black clothes, let his hair grow long, and started smoking cigarettes and marijuana.

The course of therapy for Jake and his family was long and rocky. There were many setbacks, including his dropping out of school, taking drugs, getting jailed for theft, and running away with his father's car. After his trouble with the law, his parents discontinued therapy, and I lost track of the family. I point out this particular case to demonstrate how an educated family, able to provide all the advantages to a child, can carry—from one generation to the next—attitudes and practices of discipline that are completely destructive. Of course, Mr. Grant could point out that he turned out all right and so did his other two kids. But look how inappropriate and dysfunctional his temper and frequent spankings became in the life of Jake.

Why Kids Become Aggressive

Throughout history, sages have offered many theories about why humans behave the way they do. Until recent times it was believed that most behavior was caused by supernatural forces or heredity. These approaches were used to explain misbehavior in children and aggression in adults. In contemporary times scientists have developed a number of theories to account for aggressive behavior between children and by adults toward children. Many of these theories may be used to describe attitudes and behaviors of parents toward children who misbehave. In almost thirty years of experience I have come to believe that modeling theory can best explain the way parents react to misbehavior in their children.

Modeling theory is really quite simple to understand. It is based on the belief that almost all behavior is learned by watching others. The old saying "The apple does not fall far from the tree" is true in that children learn to imitate the behavior of their parents. There is a great deal of research evidence to support this belief.

Albert Bandura, one of the major proponents of modeling theory, attempted to understand how children learn aggression. Although he and his associates acknowledged that inherited predispositions and temperament certainly account for some of personality formation, they thought most of personality is learned. In 1961, Bandura and his associates exposed nursery school children to aggressive and nonaggressive behavior, using adults as models. Children observed situations in which aggressive adults hit an inflatable plastic Bobo doll with a mallet. In addition to hitting it, the adult model yelled at the doll, sat on it, punched it, kicked it, and tossed it in the air. Another group of children watched nonaggressive play with the Bobo doll, while a third group did not view play with the doll at all. When the three groups were placed in playrooms with Bobo dolls, only those who viewed aggression against the doll became aggressive themselves.

Bandura and others went on to do other aggression studies. Most interesting are studies done by Leonard Eron, David Owens, Murry Straus, Richard Gelles, and David Gil. All these studies have demonstrated that parents who use excessive corporal punishment to the point of abuse were themselves abused. Aggression toward misbehaving children is learned in childhood from adult models. Specific incidents or patterns of abuse may be triggered by a variety of factors—parental stress, isolation, alcoholism, and so on. However, because society accepts the hitting of children, the mechanism for abuse is put in place early in life when future parents are hit themselves or observe their siblings being hit.

Leonard Eron, a research psychologist at the University of Illinois, studied 870 eight-year-olds in rural New York. He studied how severely punished they were. His indicators ranged from no physical punishment at all to slaps and spankings. He then asked other children to judge how aggressive the children in his sample were. The more aggressively children were punished, the more aggressive they were with other children. Twenty years later, Eron again studied the aggressive children as adults. It was no surprise that they had become aggressive adults with aggressive children.

Back in the late 1970s when the NCSCPA was organized, we decided to conduct a series of studies that all asked the same question: "Why do teachers assault children, physically and psychologically?" Because our major mandate was to investigate corporal punishment, we began with studies of hitting. In reviewing past records we found a great deal of research on parent-child discipline, but very little about teachers.

How Modeling Theory Explains the Views of Professionals

Because most Americans have been recipients of corporal punishment in home or school and consider it appropriate, there is a unique ethical problem for researchers and professionals interested in the area of discipline. This dilemma is especially cogent for those whose religious beliefs or personal experiences imply that corporal punishment is an effective way to deter misbehavior.

Our perceptions of appropriateness and efficacy of spanking are correlated with the frequency, intensity, duration, and context of our experiences with it as children. Given these predictors of attitude toward corporal punishment, why should one posit that anyone, including pediatricians, psychologists, and teachers, would be immune from bias when dealing with parents or when writing, reviewing, or editing articles about the subject?

For instance, should psychologists when dealing with the use of corporal punishment in schools be guided by the American Psychological Association and the National Association of School Psychologists, which have passed resolutions against the use of corporal punishment in schools? Although these organizations offer no guidelines regarding parental spanking, most child abuse experts do not look favorably upon it. For psychologists who agree with this position, practice issues may not be problematic. But what should psychologists do when working with educators and parents in the South, in rural areas, or with specific groups that consider corporal punishment to be part of their religion or culture? What if a school psychologist believes that paddling and spanking are necessary and effective in certain situations? Let me share two studies with you.

Are Psychologists Objective?

In 1983, Beth Sofer, one of my graduate students, developed a questionnaire for psychologists. We reasoned that if the education and training of teachers did not significantly reduce their use of corporal punishment, then it could be because they lacked specific in-depth training in the use of positive methods of discipline. Surely psychologists, who are highly trained regarding the use of rewards and punishments, would reflect that training in their recommendations about the use of corporal punishment. To investigate psychologists' beliefs and practices regarding corporal punishment, a random sample questionnaire was sent to psychologists all over the country.

Sofer asked the respondents to indicate what research or theory they would use to support whether or not they would recommend the use of corporal punishment. The results were surprising. While

49 percent of the respondents said they would never recommend the use of corporal punishment and accurately cited the research and theory supporting that belief, 51 percent said that in certain instances they might recommend its use. Its use might be suggested in situations that were dangerous to the child or where the misbehavior was severe and occurred repeatedly. Thirty percent said they would recommend its use in the schools.

We were surprised that so many psychologists considered it appropriate to use corporal punishment. We were even more surprised at the explanations given for recommending it. The largest group of psychologists who would recommend the use of corporal punishment cited the research of B. F. Skinner, which falls under the general category of behaviorism. This rationale was absolutely incorrect—B. F. Skinner himself repeatedly spoke and wrote about the ineffectiveness and inadvisability of the use of corporal punishment with children.

In 1995, Jeff Kaplan, another doctoral student, decided to replicate Sofer's study. He polled a random sample of psychologists from four divisions of the American Psychological Association. This time, only 23 percent of respondents said they would recommend parental use of corporal punishment (a drop of 29 percentage points from 1983). This finding is similar to another recent survey of clinical psychologists that indicated that 30 percent would suggest a spank "rarely" or "sometimes." Kaplan's study indicated that over 75 percent of the respondents opposed or strongly opposed the use of corporal punishment and that 55 percent believed spanking is an abusive act, while 8 percent felt it is child abuse. Yet 48 percent reported having used corporal punishment on their own children. Another study, by Eliza Ragsdale, showed that although 70 percent of psychologists would never recommend that a parent spank a child, 62 percent reported slapping or spanking their own child more than once. Apparently, many psychologists, as revealed in these studies, follow the old axioms such as "Believe what I say, not what I do."

Kaplan found that females were more likely to oppose the use of corporal punishment than males. Other predictors of opposition included being raised in higher rather than lower socioeconomic classes, being of Jewish religious orientation rather than Protestant or Catholic orientation, and never having received corporal punishment at home as a child. Psychologists who perceived the corporal punishment they received as a child as helpful were more likely to support and recommend the use of corporal punishment than those who perceived it as harmful, regardless of how severe the punishment. Overall, these studies suggest that beliefs do not always predict behavior even when the respondents are behavioral scientists who were mostly trained at the doctoral level.

Are Teachers Objective?

In 1982, Naomi Lennox devised a questionnaire that was administered to teachers in Pennsylvania, New York, Florida, Tennessee, and Mississippi. Teachers were asked a variety of questions about their training, their years of experience, and their own childhood. They were also asked how often they paddled their own students. The study clearly showed that teachers who paddled frequently were often spanked at home or paddled in school when they were children. Teachers who were spanked rarely or never in their own childhoods almost never paddled children. However, a small group of those who were paddled or spanked also did not use punitive techniques as teachers, a finding that has appeared in all of our studies. Why didn't modeling theory hold with this group? Another study done by one of my school psychology doctoral students may shed some light on the reasons.

How Some People Break the Cycle

In 1987, Amy Mishkin, also one of my graduate students, designed a questionnaire similar to the others I just described. However, she asked more detailed questions relating to experiences that might convince someone that hitting is a bad idea. As with the other studies, modeling theory explained most of the adults' (in this case parents') disciplining of children. However, we were most interested in the group who were hit as children but who rarely or never hit their own children. The parents in this group tended to have their children later in life. That is, they were more mature when they became parents. In addition, on a general scale of temperament and anger level, they tended to become frustrated less readily.

An interesting finding about those who were hit and did not hit is that in general they had a much higher educational level than the general population. This group and the parents who were not hit and don't hit both had educations beyond the college level. As a group they had gone to graduate and professional schools. Many reported that courses in child development and psychology had made them think about alternatives to spanking. Many had taken workshops in parenting. Another important factor was who hit them as children.

Many in the hit-no-hit group said that they were hit only by their mothers. Apparently being hit by your father or by both parents increases the chances you will become a swatting parent yourself.

Finally, the hit-no-hit parents said that a major factor in their conversions was the experience of seeing the bad effects of hitting on other children. They tended to view a swatting parent as more out of control than the misbehaving child. Obviously, this group, for a variety of reasons, had developed empathy for children. That is, they could put themselves in the shoes of the child experiencing the pain, frustration, and anger of being hit.

Parenting, Modeling, and National Character

Studies of national character offer insight into why we hit children. For instance, Germany is often thought of as an extremely aggressive country. However, Britain, with a long history of school floggings, has engaged in more wars than any modern nation. These countries both went through long periods during which children were taught reflexive obedience, order, and conformity through the use of corporal punishment.

Many Germans, especially those who have forsworn violence, believe that their culture has historically been *kinderfeindlich,* or hostile to children. Interestingly, German-speaking Austria has forbidden parental spanking, and as I write this book the German legislature is considering a similar law. Perhaps political leaders have begun to get the message that a country's disciplinary practices reflect and shape national character. This may be seen in a study conducted in the early 1970s.

Trained observers were placed in playgrounds in Germany, Denmark, and Italy. They observed aggressive acts between adults and children and between children.

In Italy and Denmark the observers noted no acts of aggression by adults against children and relatively little child-to-child aggression. In Germany there were high rates of both types of aggression. German playgrounds were characterized by pushing, kicking, fighting over toys, beatings, and aggressive pursuits. In the other playgrounds children played cooperatively and nonaggressively. This study suggests that German parents, as compared to the others, transmitted values that were based on aggression as a way to solve problems. While this one study is hardly sufficient to characterize national values, it does show the powerful effects of national traditions on parenting and perhaps national character. Unfortunately, we have no comparable studies that include the United States. But based on what I know, we would not fare well in comparison to many other countries in terms of hitting children.

Let's consider one more example of national character. Alice Miller, a psychoanalyst living in Switzerland, has written an interesting book whose German title translates literally as *In the Beginning Was Education.* The English edition is titled *For Your Own Good.* This book was widely read in Germany and may have helped to convince many policymakers that banning corporal punishment of children in all settings would enhance democratic principles in child rearing.

Miller analyzes the effect of punitiveness on individuals and societies in "lands with the kind of hidden cruelty that is so often rationalized in the time honored phrase, 'this is for your own good.'" The frequent association of corporal punishment with the demand for reflexive, unquestioning obedience is described as a major contributor to the development of character in Adolf Hitler. Miller also discloses how "poisonous pedagogy" in the home and at school contributed to a self-destructive adolescence and the development of a child murderer. She demonstrates through clinical evidence and case study what happens to children who are physically punished, humiliated, and demeaned by parents and who are "expected, indeed commanded, to respect and love those who have abused them."

In discussing Hitler, Miller explains how a child who was once persecuted becomes a persecutor. Hitler had a tyrannical, cold, cruel, and distant father, who constantly spanked him and emotionally denigrated him. Although Hitler's mother expressed concern and affection at times, she was unable or unwilling to protect him from his dictatorial father. When Hitler grew up, he had learned from his family how to be a dictator. Unfortunately, he inflicted his cruelty on the world.

The case made by Miller is obviously extreme but highly instructive. In her study she discusses the success of Hitler in the context of what she considers the punitive national character of Germans. However, there is sufficient punitiveness in the Anglo-Saxon character to account for American traditions and explain why we are so reluctant to give up corporal punishment in the schools. An examination of American schools, which reflect our society, will reveal that even though we teach the *concepts* of democracy, we seldom teach or model *processes* of democracy. In fact, among the technologically advanced countries of the world, it is the English-speaking ones that are most reluctant to give up flogging, switching, and swatting.

The majority of Americans would sooner give up three squares a day than their right to spank their children. Many derive their faith in the effectiveness of whacking kids from a source that transcends all others—the Bible. Fundamentalists and others who act from a literal interpretation of the Bible believe that if you don't hit errant children, you are denying God's command. I believe that from 30 percent to 40 percent of Americans form a hard core of conservatives committed to the use of all types of punishment as a bulwark against misbehavior and crime.

In addition to those who rely on spiritual guidance in disciplining children, others base their beliefs on tradition, their own observations, and their perceptions of the seriousness of youth misbehavior as interpreted from the media. The bottom line is that America's punitive public policy toward misbehavior, deviance, and nonconformity suggests that we are a nation of punishment junkies. Look at our addiction to building jails, our "three strikes" policies, and the spectacle of politicians falling all over each other trying to prove who is toughest on crime. Look at the level of punishment involved in our war on drugs and how ineffective it has been.

Based on several years of comparative studies of other Western democracies, I believe that we are one of the most punitive in regard to children, misbehavior, and deviance. It is this high level of punitiveness in our national character that continues our resistance to the idea of stopping corporal punishment in either schools or homes.

The source of our punitiveness is a cluster of beliefs nurtured and preserved intact through the centuries by the religious right. These beliefs are supported by conservative politicians and perpetuated by the media. Many of the same assumptions are harbored deep in the hearts of many moderates. The religious and political right's ideology is the contemporary version of the Puritans' obsession with punishment, which also led them to condone wife beating and maltreatment of sailors and prisoners. This case is ably made by Philip Greven, a noted historian from Rutgers University, in his two books, *The Protestant Temperament* and *Spare the Child*.

He presents an excellent analysis of historical factors that explain contemporary fundamentalist and evangelical beliefs.

What Spanking Does to Kids

There is much debate about the actual effects of corporal punishment. These debates center on issues of age at the time of hitting, the force with which children are hit, and the effects on long-term behavior and personality development. Rather than bore you with numerous statistics, arguments about the validity of various studies, and the fine points of each debate, I will summarize what I believe are the major effects of corporal punishment on children. But first let me share with you the results of a recent and very important scientific conference on spanking.

In February 1996, I was fortunate to be a part of a panel of experts convened by the American Academy of Pediatrics, with support from New York's Montefiore Medical Center and the U.S. Maternal and Child Health Bureau, to develop a consensus statement about the short- and long-term consequences of corporal punishment. Sharing the panel with me were distinguished social scientists and physicians representing both sides of the spanking issue. Despite heated debate and some slippage into rhetoric reflecting personal biases, we were able to produce a final statement of compromise with which we could all live. The individual papers and the consensus statement are published in a supplement to *Pediatrics*. Despite our care in crafting an objective statement of our findings, the results will most likely be distorted in the media.

In essence, the thirteen-point statement released by the group refers to spanking as defined as the use of an opened hand on the extremities or buttocks that is physically noninjurious. I believe force which causes redness, soreness or bruising is injurious and would not be acceptable to most members of the group. While the group admitted that there was little pro or con scientific evidence on the spanking of two- to five-year-olds, there was agreement that surveys and studies of older children suggest that spanking is not advisable. Even the researchers in favor of spanking admitted that noncorporal methods of discipline have been shown to be effective with children of all ages, that prevention of misbehavior should be stressed, that excessive spanking is one of many risk factors for poor outcomes in the lives of children, and that parents should never spank in anger. This may be an oxymoron, since studies of spankers and spankees indicate that some level of anger is almost always associated with spankings. Finally, the group rejected spanking and paddling in schools.

While the prospankers interpret the lack of research on the harmful effects of spanking with preschoolers as proof that it is OK, I disagree and maintain that there is no reason to ever hit a child. My summary of the research and clinical experience over 30 years follows:

- Corporal punishment should not be used in schools, since there is convincing evidence that it is a significant contributing factor to emotional, legal, and social problems.

- Frequent and harsh spanking is consistently found to be present in the lives of boys who are aggressive and disobedient, who lie, cheat, are destructive with their own and others' belongings, and who associate with friends prone to delinquency.

- Frequent and harsh spanking can cause young children to bottle up their feelings of fear, anger, and hostility. In later life these children are unusually prone to suicidal thoughts, suicide, and depression.

- Despite the age or gender of the child, the family's social class or ethnicity, whether the child was hit frequently or rarely, severely or mildly, whether there were high or low levels of interaction and affection in the home, and regardless of the degree to which specific situational variables may have mitigated the effects of the punishment, spanking consistently contributes to lowered self-esteem.

- In toddlers, many punitive approaches, including spanking, do not result in compliance, but end simply with the administration of punishment. (Studies show that preschoolers who are hit are more likely to be more impulsive and aggressive than those who are not spanked. Furthermore, toddlers can be taught, using behavioral techniques such as associating their word for pain with the street or electrical outlets, to avoid those dangerous situations. Childproofing the house and monitoring toddlers will avoid the so-called necessity of spanking to teach children to avoid danger.)

- Children who are physically punished are more likely to grow up approving of it and using it to settle interpersonal conflicts. Even children who have experienced "normal" spankings are almost three times as likely to have seriously assaulted a sibling, compared to children who were not physically disciplined.

- Contrary to popular belief, studies of corporal punishment in schools indicate that it is not used as a last resort. In fact, it is too often the first punishment for nonviolent and minor misbehaviors. Beatings for minor misbehaviors can cause many stress symptoms in children.

- Younger children are hit most often; spanking slowly decreases until late adolescence. This contributes to feelings of helplessness, humiliation, and resentment that may lead to withdrawal or aggression toward caregivers.

- Boys are hit much more frequently than girls, thereby sustaining sexual stereotypes.

- In schools, minority and poor white children receive "lickings" four to five times more frequently than middle-and upper-class white children. This contributes to racism and classism in our society.

- Regional comparisons show that the highest proportion of corporal punishment in America occurs in states in the South and Southwest. Florida, Texas, Arkansas, and Alabama have consistently been among the leaders in the frequency of hitting schoolchildren. It is unreasonable and unfair that children's location should determine the degree to which they may be legally victimized.

- Corporally punished schoolchildren, especially those with emotional and academic disabilities, have suffered all types of injuries including welts, hematomas, damage to almost all external and many internal body parts, and death.

- Studies demonstrate that eliminating corporal punishment does not increase misbehavior in home or school. Systematic use of positive alternatives, however, has been shown to decrease misbehavior significantly.

What Should We Do?

If we really want to eliminate punitiveness in our society (especially child abuse), we need to convince parents and teachers to use other techniques to shape and change children's behavior. While some would say that children are inherently bad, and that adults have a natural urge to hit children, it is just not true. Attitudes of punitiveness toward children are developed in our own childhoods. These attitudes are shaped by our parents' practices, by our religious beliefs, by national identity, and even by the region in which we live. Despite the powerful effects of modeling, there is convincing research evidence that teachers and parents can break old habits.

If we relied in other areas of life on the kinds of nonsensical assumptions used to support corporal punishment, we would still be using leeches to cure diseases and burning witches at the stake. Further, common sense would tell us that a common green mold (penicillin) could have absolutely no relation to promoting health.

I have had two interesting experiences that reflect upon this problem. The first occurred on a radio talk show in Detroit. After giving my usual pitch about why hitting children is a bad idea, one of the callers disputed my statements. She claimed to be a teacher, to have a doctoral degree, and also to teach education courses in college. After listening to her argument, I said to her, "How can you teach college students and yet ignore all of the research that is against the use of corporal punishment? Can you point to one research study that says it is beneficial for teachers to hit children?"

Her reply, considering her education and position, was quite surprising. "Research is one thing, and teaching is another. I just believe that some kids need to be hit."

The other experience was quite positive. I was conducting a two-day workshop on discipline and the effects of psychological and physical abuse by teachers. The workshop, in Panama City, Florida, was in a region noted for its high rate of paddling. During the first day of the workshop, which was attended by over 150 educators, I presented all of the research against the use of verbal and physical assaults, and I also answered practical questions and talked about alternatives. The next day, one of the participants, a guidance counselor, reported the following to the audience.

"Last night, I sat in bed talking to my five-year-old daughter. I told her that I had been at a workshop during the day and I learned that you don't have to hit little children to make them behave and that I would not spank her any more. My daughter replied, 'I'm really glad, Mommy—now I don't have to spank my children when I grow up.'"

4

Back to Basics

What You Need to Know About Effective Discipline

Before you read this chapter, you should know two things about yourself: How punitive are you? And, What is your basic orientation toward discipline?

How Punitive Are You?

I want you to fill out the scale in Exhibit 4.1, which I developed for use in parent workshops on discipline. Turn to it and complete it now—you'll get clearer results if you do it before reading the rest of the chapter. When you are finished, turn to the score sheet in Exhibit 4.2, and score yourself as directed.

Ready? Now, before I tell you why I asked you to take the Parent Punitiveness Quiz, let me give you a little background. When I first started offering discipline workshops to teachers and parents, there was always a lot of debate about the pros and cons of corporal punishment. These debates inevitably led to polarization of the audience, heated emotions, and loss of time to discuss positive methods of discipline.

To save time, I developed teacher and parent forms of the punitiveness scale and used them at the very beginning of workshops. I gave participants the range of scores at once, so they could see how punitive they were compared to their peers. I then pointed out that those with the most and least punitive scores would never

EXHIBIT 4.1 Parent Punitiveness Quiz.

The following statements represent commonly held attitudes. You will probably agree with some and disagree with others. Just react to them honestly and don't dwell overmuch on each one.

Please read each statement carefully. Then, please indicate your agreement or disagreement by circling the appropriate number according to the following code. (Or if you prefer, record your answers on a separate sheet of lined paper, numbering the lines from 1 to 27, one for each of the following statements.)

1	2	3	4	5
Strongly Agree	Mildly Agree	Neither Agree Nor Disagree	Mildly Disagree	Strongly Disagree

1. Physical punishment of children should not be allowed.
   1   2   3   4   5

2. A child should never tell an adult that the adult is wrong.
   1   2   3   4   5

3. Corporal punishment is just and necessary.
   1   2   3   4   5

4. Children are not being allowed enough freedom today.
   1   2   3   4   5

5. Corporal punishment is an effective deterrent to school discipline problems.
   1   2   3   4   5

6. Corporal punishment by parents is never justified.
   1   2   3   4   5

7. Children have a moral obligation to remain loyal to their parents, no matter what the circumstances.
   1   2   3   4   5

8. Parents have the responsibility to punish children by spanking.
   1   2   3   4   5

9. Training to comply with parental authority hinders the development of self-reliance in children.
   1   2   3   4   5

10. You can't change human nature.
    1   2   3   4   5

11. Scaring a child, now and then, by the promise of a whipping is likely to have negative emotional consequences.
    1   2   3   4   5

EXHIBIT 4.1 Parent Punitiveness Quiz, *cont'd.*

12. Loyalty on the part of children to their parents is something that parents should earn.

    1   2   3   4   5

13. Physical punishment is an effective way to control children's behavior.

    1   2   3   4   5

14. Corporal punishment should be used frequently as a method of discipline.

    1   2   3   4   5

15. Children owe their parents a great deal.

    1   2   3   4   5

16. Children are the constitutional equivalents of adults, and thus should be given the same rights.

    1   2   3   4   5

17. If you spare the rod you will spoil the child.

    1   2   3   4   5

18. Children have to earn their rights.

    1   2   3   4   5

19. Since paddling and spanking children may have negative consequences, we should discontinue the practice.

    1   2   3   4   5

20. If a child acts mean he or she needs punishment rather than understanding.

    1   2   3   4   5

21. A young child's thoughts and ideas are his own business.

    1   2   3   4   5

22. Corporal punishment is not necessary as a means of discipline.

    1   2   3   4   5

23. Children should have the opportunity to negotiate rules and consequences with their parents.

    1   2   3   4   5

24. Since corporal punishment has not eliminated disciplinary problems, society should abolish it.

    1   2   3   4   5

25. Since teachers act "in loco parentis" (in place of parents) they should be permitted to physically punish a student.

    1   2   3   4   5

26. Children should be grateful to their parents.

    1   2   3   4   5

27. When parents hit children as punishment they teach them that "might makes right."

    1   2   3   4   5

EXHIBIT 4.2 Parent Punitiveness Quiz Scoresheet.

A. On the following scoresheet, enter the numbers you used in responding to each of the questions in the Parent Punitiveness Quiz (or if you prefer, use a separate sheet of paper), then total them:

Question	Response	Question	Response
1	____	19	____
4	____	21	____
6	____	22	____
9	____	23	____
11	____	24	____
12	____	27	____
16	____		

Score for Part A = _____

B. To score the questions indicated on the next part of the scoresheet, you must adjust the response you gave on the quiz. This is for scoring purposes only—it does not change the meaning of your response. Use the following key to adjust your scores for the questions indicated below.

If you gave 1 on the quiz, record a 5.

If you gave 2 on the quiz, record a 4.

If you gave 3 on the quiz, record a 3.

If you gave 4 on the quiz, record a 2.

If you gave 5 on the quiz, record a 1.

Question	Adjusted Score	Question	Adjusted Score
2	____	14	____
3	____	15	____
5	____	17	____
7	____	18	____
8	____	20	____
10	____	25	____
13	____	26	____

Score for Part B = _____

Total score (A + B) = _____

agree, so we did not need to have them debate with each other or with me.

The higher your score, the more punitive you are. People who are highly punitive, as measured by this scale, believe that children:

- Naturally owe respect, allegiance, reflexive obedience, and loyalty to parents and other authorities
- Need to be physically punished in both home and school when they misbehave
- Are best motivated by fear
- Have too much freedom
- Are not entitled to the rights accorded adults

People who are low on punitiveness on the scale believe that children:

- Are entitled to the same rights as adults, within developmental restrictions affecting health and safety
- Should never be hit
- Have the right to plan relevant parts of their lives without undue adult intrusion
- Have the potential for goodness and achievement, which is best brought out through rewards, encouragement, and freedom to make choices
- Should never be coerced by authoritarian, punitive techniques

Of course most people will fall in the middle range and will have mixed beliefs. The average score for this scale is 67. The lowest score, that is, the least punitive I have recorded, is 30; the highest score was 114. However, 68 percent of the parents who have taken this scale fall between 49 and 85. So if your score is below 45, you are extremely nonpunitive in your attitudes toward child rearing, and if you are above 85 you are more punitive than about 84 percent of parents.

You might want to compare your score to your child's other parent or stepparent to see if your attitudes are similar. A study by Dr. Fran Kahn of upper-middle-class parents from intact families found that fathers, with an average score of 73, were more punitive than their wives, who had an average score of 66.

Studies done with the punitiveness scale for professionals indicate that principals, whose jobs are often associated with discipline, control, determining and carrying out punishments, and staff supervision, tend to have the highest, most punitive scores. Psychologists, counselors, and social workers—who are most focused on mental health, prevention, and understanding the causes of misbehavior—have the lowest, least punitive scores. Further, regional differences are apparent. Professionals and parents in the South and Southwest, where almost all states still allow the use of corporal punishment on students, come out more punitive than those in the other regions.

I believe that overly punitive disciplinary techniques cause more misbehavior than they prevent. However, the reasons for misbehavior are very complex. Misbehavior is embedded in a complex of interpersonal and environmental factors that we will now consider.

Why Kids Misbehave

Now before you become too engrossed in your score and what it means about how effective you are as a disciplinarian, I want to tell you that good behavior is not only a function of what you do as a parent. I know, I know! Everyone blames parents for everything their kids do wrong. But you will be happy to hear that there are many other forces that may affect how a child behaves. The next time a teacher tells you or implies that you are the major reason why your kid is bad in school, you can ask some hard questions. While it may be true that you have made mistakes, you may not be the only reason your child misbehaves. Here are some other reasons that have been documented.

Most major misbehavior ranging from minor offenses to criminal misconduct occurs during adolescence and young adulthood.

Therefore, the size of the cohort of children born each year will generally predict the crime rate and the rate of school misbehavior fifteen years later. What happens is that the resources available to provide for youth are inadequate from the time the children need quality day care until they need recreational and vocational services from the schools and various agencies.

Current projections, based on recent birthrates, indicate that schools and the justice system can expect an epidemic of crime and misbehavior by the year 2005. This will be a tough time for parents, who will need more support and help with their kids, especially in relation to controlling peer influences.

We pay a price for extending childhood and adolescence. Adolescents' social and economic dependency on parents in modern society—especially compared to their lesser degree of dependency in all pretechnological societies—is often incongruent with their physical maturity. This extended period of adolescence, reinforced by youth-oriented media, advertising, and manufacturing, has created an adolescent peer culture that is driven by the need to be different from adults. Sometimes these needs extend to opposition and aggression against mainstream adult values.

A variety of factors can converge in adolescence to cause misbehavior. These include poor self-esteem brought on by not feeling as competent as the "normal" students in a school, in a neighborhood where the teenager lives, or among the friends he or she makes in shared activities ranging from sports to smoking pot. These can all lead to association with peers whose norms and values are contrary to those you have stressed in your home. For instance, once adolescents embrace the values of the drug culture, nothing you do—short of sending them to an isolated island—can prevent them from finding druggie friends.

Even Schools Can Contribute to Misbehavior

When schools violate individual rights, overstress conformity and obedience, and discourage creativity and dissent, they can foster rebellion among some segments of the student population. Schools governed by ineffective or authoritarian principals are most likely to have high rates of misbehavior, disruption, and violence. Overly punitive, rigid teachers can cause problems, especially when the curriculum is too hard or too easy for individual students or when homework demands or dull work become excessive. Misbehavior-plagued schools may implement ineffective and inane rules, emphasize competition over cooperation, and inappropriately violate students' rights.

Often teachers unwittingly create problems by not communicating adequately with parents. They may believe that parents either don't discipline children adequately or don't care enough. Blaming parents does not solve the problem. Further, some teachers with considerable discipline problems are often their own worst enemies because of their refusal to examine how their own classroom behavior causes discipline problems.

Teachers' failures to maintain discipline often contribute to burnout, which renders them even more incapable of controlling classes. Poor instruction may account for over 50 percent of classroom misbehavior. Further, emotional maltreatment by educators is a major cause of student anger, alienation, and rebellion. It includes verbal assaults, putdowns, ridicule, isolation and rejection, punitive sanctions, peer humiliation, and sexual corruption.

Federal laws mandate that local schools place every child with disabilities in the "least restrictive environment." If the least restrictive environment for a misbehaving student is deemed to be the regular classroom, the teacher must deal with a student who is thoroughly unwelcome in the class. Further, current inclusion legislation, which may result in children with severe behavior problems being placed in regular classrooms without sufficient resources, may have a tremendous impact on teacher attitudes about misbehavior. If full inclusion of these students is mandated without sufficient funding for support services, misbehavior in regular classes will increase and regular teachers will need to develop more expertise in dealing with misbehavior.

Youth unemployment and lack of summer employment for over 50 percent of minority inner-city adolescents and large numbers of rural youth, many of whom are school dropouts, reflect our society's failure to prevent associated misbehavior and delinquency. Many unemployed adolescents feel helpless and hopeless about their futures. With little chance of their legitimately earning money in a society driven by consumerism, is there any question why so many turn their frustration against others?

Family Factors

Family problems such as divorce and economic stress can contribute to misbehavior. If both parents in a divorce are involved in parenting, misbehavior is likely if parents are not consistent in discipline styles. For instance, a guilt-ridden parent who left the home may be overly permissive and indulgent with the children. As a consequence, the other parent must enforce limits. These problems may spill over into the school. Economic stress on families may exacerbate existing disciplinary problems or create the conditions for misbehavior.

When working reduces the time available for their own children, parents are less likely to volunteer to lead community groups such as Scouts or Little League. Hard-pressed municipalities have fewer resources to support supervised recreational programs, and good day care is often available only to those who can afford it. Many children lose access to programs that contribute to self-discipline, help develop good coping skills and positive self-esteem, inculcate a sense of responsibility to the community, and provide productive uses of free time.

Additionally, there is sufficient evidence that television can cause or exacerbate behavior problems. Frequent television viewing decreases social gatherings away from home, community activities, family conversations, and household care. It also results in depressed reading ability and may encourage aggressive and undesirable behavior. For instance, unrealistic fight scenes from movies ranging from Power Rangers to Bruce Lee sagas may convince children that people who are punched in the face, hit over the head with baseball bats, or slammed head-first into walls do not sustain cuts, concussions, bruises, broken bones, and serious internal injuries.

Finally, kids who misbehave must take responsibility for the consequences of what they do. There are two sides to this coin. Chronic failure to accept responsibility can result from either of two opposing errors in upbringing. First, children who are psychologically or physically abused at an early age or throughout their upbringing have a good chance of becoming aggressive, hostile, and distrustful of all adults and most peers. These children have parents who never, or inconsistently, model love, affection, and caring. Their parents may be abusive alcoholics, rigidly militaristic in administering rules, mentally disturbed, or religious zealots. These children may not develop a conscience as we know it because they are incapable of empathy. They lie, cheat, and hurt others without compunction. They will never accept blame and always try to fault others for what they did. At the extreme end of the continuum is the psychopath, who can never be cured.

Second are the children raised with complete lack of limits as a result of overly permissive parenting. These children never experience any consequences for their misbehavior. They also can lack empathy, be very immature and self-centered, and expect the world to revolve around them. Despite parental expressions of love, they are never taught to give love, and in many way are just as damaged as the abused children.

Now that we have considered a variety of causes of misbehavior, let us examine how you personally perceive its causes and cures. Your perceptions are greatly influenced by your orientation to discipline.

What Is Your Orientation to Discipline?

While your beliefs and behaviors regarding punitiveness are important, they are mediated by your beliefs about child rearing in general. It is thus useful to turn to your basic beliefs, philosophies, and experiences regarding how children develop and why they misbehave. I believe there are factors that differentiate people's understandings of how to discipline children. This is completely spelled out in a textbook for teachers that I recently completed with several associates, *School Discipline and School Violence: The Teacher Variance Approach*. While the material in that book is focused on how to diagnose, prevent, and remediate classroom misbehavior, the basic concepts are relevant to anyone who wants to discipline children.

The following paragraphs present a brief overview so that you can identify your own orientation within the five models I propose. I will cover the first four approaches quickly. If you want to become an expert in a particular approach, you can start by reading my text on teacher variance. In this book, I will be concentrating on the Ecological-Systems Approach to deal with discipline.

The *Behavioral* and *Cognitive-Behavioral Approaches* are based on behavioral theory, which posits that all behavior is learned. If you favor this orientation you believe:

- Behavior, feelings, thoughts, and beliefs are learned.

- All learning occurs as a function of principles of reinforcement and punishment.

- Reinforcement is the most powerful shaper of behavior.

- Behavior, thoughts, and feelings can be reported, measured, predicted, and controlled.

- Behavior can be modified through systematic reinforcement, withdrawal of reinforcement, punishment, and rational persuasion.

- New behaviors, thoughts, feelings, and beliefs can be learned to replace those that are irrational, self-destructive, and self-defeating. This may be done by use of reinforcement, self-talk, rehearsal, and practice. You can, by following basic principles of behaviorism and cognitive-behavioral theory, unlearn misbehaviors and learn appropriate behaviors.

The *Psychodynamic-Interpersonal Approach* is based on the assumption that all personality and behavior develop as a result of interactions with significant others during crucial developmental stages. If you are strong in this approach, you believe:

- Personality and behavior are strongly influenced by inherent, genetically programmed drives and needs.
- Various drives and needs emerge at specific developmental stages.
- Personality is shaped by the nature of the interaction with parents and significant others during each stage.
- Misbehavior may occur if children and youth do not make adequate adjustments during each developmental stage.
- The nature and quality of parenting during the stages of development up to about five or six years of life are crucial in determining later adjustment.
- Misbehavior is often the result of patterns of inadequate or deviant parenting passed from one generation to another.
- Misbehavior is almost always associated with poor self-image and low self-esteem.
- Misbehavior is often a function of behavior that has not matured during a particular developmental period or of inadequate ability to handle anxiety.

The *Humanistic Approach* is rooted in the belief that all people are inherently good and responsible for their destinies. This approach leads you to believe:

- All people are born with an inherent capacity for empathy, caring, curiosity, spontaneity, and goodness, and strive toward being competent, loved, and self-actualized.
- All children have an innate desire to learn.

- Children's desires to learn are stifled when parents and schools frustrate their unique needs, their individual learning styles, and their need to become competent in their own way.

- Bureaucracies such as schools, which are organized in hierarchical, authoritarian structures, suppress individuality, unique styles of self-expression, and self-actualization.

- Misbehavior occurs when children are not allowed to learn in their own ways or to express and fulfill their unique needs without hurting others.

- Misbehavior occurs in school when students rebel against the unjust authority and tyranny of meaningless rules, regulations, and curricula.

- Participatory democracy should be taught as a process in homes and schools.

- The focus of education at home and in school should be on the process and joy of learning, rather than on memorizing and regurgitating specific course contents and facts in order to pass tests.

If you are high in Humanism you probably also had a low score on the survey at the beginning of the chapter, indicating that you are less punitive than the norm.

The *Heredity and Biophysical Factors Approach* is based on the belief that biology is destiny. It leads you to believe:

- Everyone is born with genetically determined traits such as intelligence, athletic ability, and temperament.

- Behavior is adversely affected when individuals are not in an optimal state of health.

- Misbehavior may be caused by biologically based disorders of affect, attention, or learning or by inherited vulnerabilities such as alcoholism.

- Misbehavior may be the result of unidentified physical disabilities such as visual impairment, auditory impairment, hor-
  monal imbalance, or disorders of metabolism.
- Misbehavior may be the result of inadequate nutrition.
- Misbehavior may be the result of ingestion of inappropriate
  substances.

An Ecological-Systems Approach to Discipline

Most child psychologists adhere more or less to one of the four
approaches I have described. If you have occasion to seek help for
your child, you might want to ask about the psychologist's basic orientation. Despite this tendency to choose a basic orientation, however, more experienced psychologists often find that techniques
from different approaches work in specific situations. Therefore,
they become eclectic in their practice. An eclectic approach is
rooted in a theory that is best described as a fifth approach I call the
Ecological-Systems Approach, which is what we will discuss in the
rest of this book.

The *Ecological-Systems Approach* is based on the belief that:

- Misbehavior cannot be completely explained by one single
  theory of personality development.
- Misbehavior is the result of an ongoing complex interaction of
  all ecological and interpersonal forces within the system that
  includes the child's total life experiences with every aspect of
  the environment.
- Misbehavior can be caused by dysfunction between the child
  and any particular system in the environment.
- The appropriateness or deviancy of most behaviors is a function of the setting and is not inherent in the behavior itself.
- Alienation, underachievement, and misbehavior can be successfully addressed through appropriate modifications in parenting and teaching styles and techniques.

- Individual misbehavior must be understood as a dysfunction between parent or teacher and child, not just of the child alone.

- Misbehavior can be perpetuated by stereotyping and inaccurate assumptions about the child's role identification.

- The real solution to discipline problems is within the family system rather than in the individual.

Without being aware of it, you probably use this approach in your administration of discipline. That is, what you do reflects all of your previous experiences, observations, and expectations with each of your children in different settings. It is a common sense, pragmatic, experiential approach to discipline. In healthy families, parents do the things to children that made them feel good and behave when they themselves were children. Remember the modeling effect?

If your family is running well, all family members know their boundaries and limitations. They all give and feel entitled to their share of love, attention, and praise. You are neither overly permissive or overly punitive. When trying to understand misbehavior you will consider all relevant factors including the child's internal forces such as needs, drives, innate temperament, biological urges, and physiological conditions, and the external forces such as siblings, how your family functions, reinforcers, punishers, peers, and the physical setting of your home. Rather than taking misbehavior as a personal and direct affront to your integrity and worth as a parent, you will view the misbehavior as part of a system—that is your family, the neighborhood, and the school.

The setting designates what is "normal" and "abnormal." For instance, for a ten-year-old, trying out dirty words with a peer group is different from trying them out on you while you have guests at dinner. In this latter case, a punishment might be in order—but how will punishment keep a child from cursing in the secrecy of a tight circle of peers?

You know never to label your kid as bad, because this becomes a self-fulfilling prophecy. That is, if you treat children as if they are bad, they will come to believe they are bad and therefore act as bad kids. This leads us to the concept of prevention. We will talk more about what to do about misbehavior in the rest of this book.

An Ounce of Prevention

I believe I have rallied enough evidence to convince most readers that spanking is a bad idea. However, you may still be waffling on whether or not it is *always* a bad idea. After all, I am sure that you have heard some "experts" say that in certain situations, like when little Johnny is inclined to run out into the street, a good smack on the behind will change his mind. Well, I am here to tell you that you never have to hit your children. Ever. I am going to share the basics of discipline with you and tell you how to begin.

In real estate there is a saying you may have heard. The value of real estate is determined by location, location, and location. I believe that the most valuable aspect of a total discipline program is prevention, prevention, and prevention. The idea is to prevent misbehavior from occurring by providing the type of environment that nurtures well-behaved, productive children within the context of our democratic society. What does this mean in terms of what you must do?

Meeting Children's Needs

I believe that psychologist Abraham Maslow best described the needs you must fulfill for your child to be well behaved. From the beginning, infants need to be well nourished and safe from physical and emotional harm. To me, this means feeding on demand, lots of hugging, caressing, and skin contact between baby and parents, and lots of loving, soft sounds and cooing from caregivers. Infants' needs are pretty easy—at least in terms of figuring out what to do, exhausting as it may be to do it. Toddlers, however, require both satisfaction and a sense of structure and limit setting, and that requires more thought on your part.

The discipline of toddlers and young children must always be done in an atmosphere that provides for the child's developing needs for affection, affiliation, and love. Young children need the feeling of unconditional positive regard from parents. This means that when they misbehave and are admonished, you must communicate that you still love them but you don't like the misbehavior. For example, when Jimmy smacks his sister, he needs to hear you say, "Jimmy, I really love you, but hitting your sister is not allowed, and if you do it again I will have to punish you," rather than, "Jimmy, you are a terrible bully for hitting your sister. What is the matter with you? You do that again and I will smack you."

From toddlerhood through adult life children must gradually learn to master the world in terms of physical demands such as those required to play sports and intellectual demands such as those made at school and work. If children are not able to fulfill their needs for intellectual and physical control, they will develop poor self-esteem, a precursor to much misbehavior.

Since the California schools made the building of self-esteem a goal of education, the concept has taken a beating from all sorts of right-wing ideologists. But I want to tell you, in my thirty years as a psychologist, I have never seen a child with good self-esteem referred because of misbehavior. Nor have I ever seen an adult patient with depression or anxiety disorder who didn't have problems with self-esteem. Research by Murry Straus and others offers clear evidence that spanking consistently contributes to lowered self-esteem, depression, and other emotional problems.

In childhood and adolescence, children will need to feel affiliation and love with parents, peers, and various role models. You need to provide for all of these. But this may be quite difficult. For instance, you may not like fifteen-year-old Sam's affiliation with Judy, who smokes and wears baggy clothes. But Sam's need to differentiate from his parents, his need to explore another type of love from parent-child love, his need to feel some sense of independence—not to mention his biological needs—may all put you in the back seat. Suddenly you find you are no longer in total control. So should you absolutely forbid him to see Judy? Or should you reason and negotiate and not show your total dislike for Judy and everything you think she stands for? Of course, if you are rich enough to send him to a private school in Europe, you may never hear about Judy again. But if—like most parents—you can't control all aspects of your teenager's life (the bus ride to and from school, the people he hangs out with in school, the way he spends some or much of his after-school and weekend time), you may have to negotiate and compromise your dislike of Judy and your anger at Sam's defiance.

Depending on individual circumstances, children and adolescents will have varying needs for justice, goodness, beauty, order, and unity. I have seen some very bright young adolescents who absolutely feel that they are entitled to all of the rights of adults as part of their need for total justice in their lives. That is, they expect parents and schools to always explain and justify rules and to offer strong support for why the rules are needed. These kids act as if they are lawyers or judges, weighing whether rules are rational, fair, and just. If they feel the rules are unjust they unilaterally decide not to obey them.

For instance, President Clinton and Congress have supported the concept that uniforms will help reduce school violence, engender more respect for adults, and make schools safer. Yet there is not a shred of scientific evidence to support this reworked version of a concept long ago discredited scientifically, politically, and pedagogically by public schools. Further, whenever the rule is implemented, there will be some students and parents who will periodically challenge the uniform requirement on constitutional grounds.

Some students and parents believe that making everyone wear uniforms is antithetical to the democratic system. They will not buy into the pragmatic reasoning behind the rule, such as saving money on clothes and keeping richer kids from feeling superior to their less well dressed peers who can't afford designer clothes. Rather than worrying about what students wear, legislators would be better off voting for sufficient funds to enable schools to use proven techniques to improve discipline and avoid violence. These include the reduction in both school and class size, adequate and updated curriculum materials and supplies, sufficient tutorial, remedial, and mental health services, and quality inservice training in discipline and school safety for teachers and administrators. It would also be useful to provide safe passage for students both to and from school and to employ principals who are fair, consistent, and available to students and parents. You see, prevention will work just as well at the school level as it does with individual families. Besides adequate resources, prevention requires patient and informed caregivers. However, many are seduced by the lure of punishment, which costs very little money, results in immediate cessation of misbehavior, and requires no training, even though it is generally effective only in the short term.

But I am not asking you to be the perfect parent—I recognize that there is no such thing. Even in the best of circumstances we can't always protect, provide for, and be there for our children. Economic restraints, limited availability of competent and nurturing caregivers, scarcity of quality time with your child, your child's biologically determined temperament, your child's intellectual, neurological, or emotional disability, and a host of other factors may make it difficult to meet all your child's needs. We all make mistakes, but we can all learn from them. We can always strive to do the right thing, and that almost always pays off. You can begin with the basic dos and don'ts of effective prevention.

The Dos and Don'ts of Prevention

So how can you raise mentally healthy kids who can balance obedience with independence, conformity with self-expression, respect for authority with questioning of authority, self-love with love for others, and need to achieve with need to play? How can your children, in a very difficult and always changing world, develop creativity, enthusiasm, a lust for life, a sense of well-being, and a striving for competence? Here are some parental basics that are pre-requisites to effective prevention of misbehavior. This is just a general overview—the rest of the book will deal with the specifics of how to deal with misbehavior.

What You Must Do

If you completely and competently adhere to the dos and don'ts that follow, you are a perfect parent. But don't worry; there are no perfect parents, or at least there are not any I have observed. The stress of contemporary parenthood makes it all too easy to lose it more than you want. But if you adhere to the spirit and philosophy inherent in these guidelines, you will do just fine.

- *Do make sure that your child or adolescent understands that you are the parent.* You can and should negotiate, explain, and share decision making with your child, but ultimately you may have to set the limits and enforce the rules.
- *Do catch your kid being good.* Whenever appropriate, praise, reward, and encourage your child for good behavior.
- *Do use soft reprimands rather than harsh threats.* If you depend mostly on reward and praise, you rarely have to punish children, especially those at the preschool level. With generally well-behaved children, it is often sufficient to merely suggest the threat of some unknown punishment when the child misbehaves. For instance, you can say, "Rachael, you better stop doing that by the time I count to three, or else. OK, one . . . (pause for a few seconds), two . . . (pause for another few seconds), and . . ." By the time you have counted to two, Rachael has imagined all sorts of dire consequences for her misbehavior and promptly complies with your request. Because children like Rachael rarely misbehave, they are not familiar with punishments and can only think that some horrible fate is in store if they don't comply. Because they always comply, they never find out what terrible consequences lie in wait. Of course, by

the time they are five or six, they begin to realize that their parents would never give them a horrible punishment. However, just in case Rachael does test the limits to the count of three, be prepared to swiftly place her in time-out or to follow through with the loss of some privilege.

- *Do teach your child to express emotions verbally.* Teach five-year-old Davey to say, "Mommy, I'm angry that you said that to me. You hurt my feelings." This is better than for him to express his anger through negative behavior.

- *Do model the behavior you want.* If you don't want thirteen-year-old Sarah to smoke, don't model smoking.

- *Do have patience.* If you have a temper problem, read Chapter Seven and follow my suggestions. If this doesn't work, get help.

- *Do hug, kiss, and cuddle your children at least once a day.* Frequently tell them that you love them and are proud of them. Model appropriate public displays of affection with your spouse in front of your children. This includes spontaneous hugs and kisses and verbal expressions of fondness and regard.

- *Do, from the earliest possible age, begin teaching empathy, cooperation, and rational problem solving.* Convince your child to do the right thing because it is the right thing to do, not because of fear of punishment.

- *Do try to develop a relatively consistent parenting plan with your spouse.* At an early age, children will recognize that they can play one parent against the other.

- *Do track your child for developmental milestones.* Recognize the appropriate or inappropriate emergence of expected behaviors such as walking and talking and misbehaviors such as temper tantrums and sibling rivalry. There are a number of good books that will help you to understand simple facts about when temper tantrums may occur, when to expect bed wetting to stop, and why preteens begin to not want to be seen in certain places with you. Because that is a topic beyond the scope of this book, you can refer to any of the books I have listed in the Resources and Further Reading section. You may consider this your first homework assignment in becoming an expert in discipline if you are just starting out as a parent.

As early as possible, if you see problems, trust your gut feelings and don't listen to advice that your child will "grow out of it" if that advice doesn't seem consistent with what you observe over time. I can't overstress the importance of early detection of medical, neurological, intellectual, or emotional problems. Problems such as hearing impairment, Attention-Deficit Hyperactivity Disorder, and learning disabilities, if not treated early, frequently lead to behavior problems. Keep track of your child's developmental progress and know what questions to ask your pediatrician. If you are not happy with the answer, always take your child to specialists such as speech and hearing specialists, pediatric neurologists, or school or child psychologists.

• *Do recognize transgenerational parenting that is ineffective.* Above all others, know thyself. Unless you have taken specific courses in parenting, you are probably disciplining your child as you were disciplined. So think about how you were disciplined as a child. Think back to the way you felt about the rewards and punishments meted out by your parents. Are you unconsciously using the same ineffective phrases and admonitions that infuriated you when your parents repeated them over and over? You probably learned to tune them out so that they had no effect whatsoever. So why are you surprised and hurt when your kids tune you out?

• *Do your best to be objective.* Use humor and don't always take yourself seriously. You don't have to be God to your child. You will make mistakes, but be able to step back and see the humor in them.

• *Do use rational, moral persuasion to teach children to behave appropriately.* Although you don't always have to give children reasons for why they should behave in a certain way, do it as much as you can. Of course, after repeated discussions, you may sometimes have to say, "You must do it because I say so. I am your parent, I love you, and I know best." However, if you have done a good job of instilling self-discipline and internal controls in your child, you should rarely, if ever, have to resort to this type of *power assertion* parenting.

- *Do set limits and provide structure.* Make sure that your child knows what behaviors are unacceptable, and make sure that you respond consistently when rules are broken. Children should also know how highly you value specific acceptable behaviors. Some parents and teachers post rules and consequences and desirable behaviors so that there is no question about them.
- *Do encourage your children to watch educational television.* Watch with them when the shows teach children moral messages or the stories leave open the possibility to discuss the moral or immoral behaviors of the characters. Follow through with your own discussions to reenforce the messages.
- *Do monitor your child's television viewing.* Prevent or limit viewing of programs that present violent solutions to problems.

What You Should Not Do

I'll bet that without reading what follows you know perfectly well what you should not do. But just like me, you are sometimes too irritable, cranky or just plain tired to do the right thing. Few of us are 100 percent, so just try as hard as you can to avoid making these discipline mistakes.

- *Do not ever threaten a punishment that you are not prepared to carry out.*
- *Do not ever compare children.* The worst thing you can say to Billy is, "Why can't you be as good as your brother? He never gives me any aggravation."
- *Do not scold, scream, or psychologically put down your child.* Emotional maltreatment consists of sarcasm, ridicule, name calling, putdowns, and scapegoating.
- *Do not let yourself get out of control while punishing a behavior.* Walk away first if possible, and then come back when you are rational.

If you can apply the basic dos and don'ts of prevention, you may not even have to read the rest of this book. You may only be

interested in discussions of how to handle misbehaviors that typically end in spankings. But the truth is, few of us can be perfect parents—so you may want to read the rest anyway.

You Can Do It

Now, before we go any further, let me be honest with you. Rational,
informed, and positive discipline is not easy. It takes understanding, patience, and humor. You need to have a general understanding
about why children misbehave. So if you think anyone can spoon-
feed you a few simple messages as I have just done and that it will
then be easy to raise kids, I am sorry to disappoint you. But now you
have the basics of prevention and positive discipline techniques—
if you study and apply them persistently, consistently, and carefully,
you will be successful.

I know it is tough. Any parent knows that you can read all the
books on development, discipline, and parenting, but none can
completely prepare you for the job. No one reading this book lives
in a simple society, where people's roles are decided at birth and
where there are relatively few options. Don't believe those promot-
ers of the need to return to so-called traditional values. We are no
longer hunter-gatherers, agrarian tillers of the soil, or members of
the unchanging industrial society portrayed in the nostalgia for the
fifties. Besides, in America, the "good old days" when kids respected
their parents were really bad old days for many kids, wives, and families. Historians know that those were days of great numbers of
unreported and unpunished cases of wife and child abuse. Not to
mention the gross psychological damage done to minority children
and adolescents growing up in segregated America. Despite the age-
old prophecies of doom and gloom from the religious right, spare us
a return to the good old days when family values were controlled by
men who virtually owned their wives and children.

Now after what I have said, don't lose heart. I am going to continue to tell you what you need to know about discipline. These are
the basics as I understand them after thirty years as a researcher,

practitioner, and parent. After reading this you will know what you have to face and how to face it. You may not know all the answers, but you will know where to find them or how to get help.

After considering how punitive you are, the next thing to do is to determine if your level is too high. If it is, only you know why and only you can change. Think about your orientation to discipline and how it can be applied to the things I discuss here. Next, you must accept that because human behavior is complex, the reasons for misbehavior are complex. There is always a reason why a child misbehaves. Each of the orientations helps you to understand why a child misbehaves, but there is always a reason.

Some causes of misbehavior are quite simple to understand and some are more difficult. But in most discipline situations, you begin with an advantage that you may forget that you have. You know a lot more about being a child, getting along in the world, and a lot of other related issues about human behavior than your child does. With some effort, you can always figure out what is going on. I find that most parents who have difficult children, with a little help from me, really do understand the problem. The problem is that they can't think and act rationally about what their child is doing "to them."

So by now you have some understanding of why children misbehave and the basics of good discipline. You know how punitive you are in comparison to other parents, you have some idea about the different orientations to discipline, you are aware of the importance of prevention, and you have a good idea about the causes of misbehavior. Many of those causes can be explained within the four theoretical frameworks I discussed. If interested, you can read more about those particular approaches. However, I have chosen the ecological-systems approach to help you deal with misbehavior because this approach can encompass all the others. Because it's not bound by a narrow theory, you can pick and choose how to diagnose and remediate a particular problem.

5

Changing Your Approach to Discipline

In the previous chapter, I discussed the many causes of misbehavior. You now know that because behavior is complex, misbehavior is also complex. Therefore the first thing you must do to deal with misbehavior once it has occurred is to try to understand what caused it. Think of yourself as a discipline doctor. You must diagnose the disease before you can prescribe a cure.

Diagnose the Causes of the Misbehavior

Mrs. Rodriguez called to refer her son, nine-year-old Fernando, for counseling. She indicated that Fernando had been talking back to his teacher, refusing to do homework, and doing everything possible to avoid going to school. He procrastinated with his chores at home and was beginning to be fresh to her. She felt desperate and said that she needed help in disciplining her son. She just didn't know what to do since neither of her other two children ever acted this way.

At the first interview with Fernando and his parents, he impressed me as a polite, sensitive nine-year-old, with at least average intelligence. His parents were hard-working, serious people. This intact working-class family lived in a modest suburban community and stated that they moved there from the city so that their children could get a good education.

When I asked what the parents did when Fernando refused to do what he was told, Mrs. Rodriguez said she asked him five or six times and usually ended up screaming at him. Obviously, that wasn't effective or she wouldn't have come for help. Mr. Rodriguez said that he only asked Fernando to do something once. If there was any hint of refusal or show of disrespect, Fernando knew he would immediately get smacked. This seemed effective, since Fernando rarely directly defied his father.

It was clear that Mr. and Mrs. Rodriguez were relying on punishment to discipline Fernando. Up until last year Fernando had been relatively well behaved. Given the information I had, I could have dealt with the problem on a surface level without probing for the underlying causes or the function of Fernando's oppositional behavior.

I could easily have helped these parents set up a behavioral program focusing on rewards for good behavior. I am sure there would have been an improvement. But after all these years as a parent and psychologist, there is no question in my mind that all misbehavior serves some purpose. In this case we had a change in behavior that had to be caused by some change in the environment, because there didn't appear to be evidence of any change in the family or in Fernando's health or development that might have caused the problem. When routine disciplinary techniques that worked in the past become ineffective, it is crucial to determine the cause of the misbehavior before turning to new or more intense forms of punishment. Obviously, more screaming and spanking had not motivated Fernando to stop his oppositional behavior.

A two-hour family interview revealed that Fernando was always a polite, hard-working kid until he got into 4th grade. Then his behavior started to change. He claimed his teacher was mean, that she embarrassed him by making him read out loud, that the written tests were too long to finish, and that she gave him too much homework. Bingo! I had a working hypothesis about why Fernando was having problems. I focused on the hypothesis that Fernando's change in behavior might be related to some type of undiagnosed learning problem.

Why did I guess that he might have a learning problem? Well, first, here was a well-behaved, hard-working boy who got passing grades through 3rd grade. In these primary grades children spend much time on learning the basics of reading and math. Only the most sensitive and knowledgeable teachers in these grades will notice anything when a polite, nice-looking child encounters a minor learning problem. But in 4th grade, where the students begin to use their skills to read and write a lot more, some kids with minor learning problems start to have difficulties that can not be ignored.

When I asked how Fernando felt about himself, his parents mentioned that he had begun making self-disparaging statements such as, "I am stupid, no one likes me," and "Sometimes I wish I wasn't born." Bingo, again. Fernando's self-doubts and fears of being stupid began when he was put into the lowest reading group, had trouble copying assignments and writing paragraphs, and began to recognize that other kids were doing much better than he was.

The family revealed that Fernando's older brother had been diagnosed with a learning disability in 1st grade. But because his problem was so severe, they never connected his problem with Fernando's misbehavior. When I asked both parents if they had any problems in school, I got a mixed genetic message. Mrs. Rodriguez graduated from high school and enjoyed reading. However, Mr. Rodriguez, who dropped out of school when he was sixteen, never enjoyed reading. He said he had trouble learning to read, and it wasn't until he was an adult that he felt he could read well enough to master the sports page of the newspaper. Further, he reported that his father was an intelligent man but was basically illiterate.

Reviews of Fernando's school records showed that he had slow reading ability and poor writing and spelling skills. It seemed that instead of facing the embarrassment of constant failure and proof that he was stupid, he shifted everyone's attention to his misbehavior. It was now clear that the purpose of his misbehavior was to avoid schoolwork that he couldn't do.

Fortunately, the school was cooperative, which is not always the case when children have mild disabilities that may not be severe enough for official classification. With his parents present, I explained to Fernando that he was not stupid, that he had a specific disability that he shared with some famous people, and that the school would help him to adjust to his problem. I made sure he realized that it was not his fault and that he could succeed, but that he would have to work a little harder than other kids.

In school his writing assignments were minimized, especially in terms of homework. He was allowed to take tests orally in science and social studies, because he really had trouble with writing under timed circumstances. His parents, who felt guilty for punishing him so much, agreed to stop their ineffective punishments. We set up a behavioral program of rewards for good schoolwork, and all parties agreed that he would only come to his mother for help with his homework when he needed it. She would stop bugging him.

In this case the cause of the misbehavior was the boy's learning problem. Attention to that was the primary reason why his behavior improved dramatically after the problem was addressed. Now, I do not expect you to be a psychologist and be able to test your child. However, you can learn to recognize when you need help and when you don't.

If you are tuned to each of your children's personalities, you have taken the first step in diagnosis. You will be able to recognize even subtle shifts in mood and behavior. If these shifts continue or result in sudden and dramatic change, you will be able to immediately investigate causes. If you have good communication with your child, you will be able to get accurate information from the child. If you have to nag and wheedle to get information, then communication is not so good or the child is too embarrassed to discuss the topic with you. However, even in the latter cases, if you are close to your child you will be able to figure out what happened.

Another signpost of trouble occurs when a child is unresponsive to the usual motivators and punishments, as was the case with Fernando. If a child discontinues misbehavior after use of regular preventive and punishment techniques, the cause of his misbehavior is probably not complicated. However, when the usual techniques do not work, you have to begin to think in more complex ways about the meaning or function of his misbehavior. Here is where you need to examine all the possible causes. In the following section I offer you some ideas about how to gather enough information to make your own hypotheses about why your child is not responding to the techniques that used to work.

How to Observe Your Child Systematically

There is no substitute for directly observing a child's appropriate and inappropriate behavior across a variety of situations in order to understand the causes of the misbehavior. Professionals use formal observation instruments, checklists, and audio- and videotapes for the purpose, aiming to obtain an ongoing record of all the factors that surround a misbehavior. As a parent, you would generally not have access to these instruments or the time and training to use them properly. However, some professional techniques can easily be adapted for home use. Let me give you an example.

Eight-year-old Jill and Cindy, her six-year-old sister, generally get along well. However, when Jill's friend Alice comes over to play, there is constant squabbling. After Alice leaves, the fighting continues for several days. You suspect that this is Alice's fault, but you are not sure what she is doing. You suspect that Jill wants to avoid playing with her little sister when Alice is present because Jill doesn't want to play baby games in front of her peers. When you ask Jill about this she denies it and just says that Jill is always butting in and that Alice is nice to her and one of her best friends in school. You decide to observe their behavior directly. You can do this by writing short descriptions of incidents that are both positive and negative. These are called *anecdotal records*, because they report in short anecdotes.

First you get a *baseline* by writing down some descriptions of Jill and her sister playing together. It is called a baseline because it provides information about behaviors before the variable that may cause the problem is introduced into the situation. An example of a baseline would be how you normally feel before you take a particular medicine. It gives you a point or points to compare with how you feel while on the medicine. With Jill and Cindy, you might decide to write down at least one incident each day for a week. These will take place when Alice is not there. For example:

> Saturday—March 22—10:15 A.M. Jill is watching TV. She is lying on her back on the floor. Cindy comes in with Candy Land and asks Jill to play with her. Jill says she will, but Cindy must wait until the show is over. She invites Cindy to watch with her, and after the show is over they play Candy Land. They get along fine.

After making a number of anecdotal reports, you can look for recurring patterns. From the reports taken on Jill and Cindy it became clear that the recurring pattern is that Jill is willing to play with her sister and that she is a very good negotiator. She is teaching Cindy to compromise and to wait to get what she wants. This is your baseline for how the two children play together. Next, you decide to watch them play when Alice is there and to write down incidents.

These reports soon show that Alice has never learned to compromise. She is angry at her bossy older sister. When she plays with Cindy, she assumes the role of the bossy older sister and expects Jill to do the same. This is the recurring pattern. Further anecdotes may show that it is easier for Jill to give in to Alice than to try to mediate between Alice and Cindy. After Alice leaves, Cindy is mad at her older sister for a few days and makes it difficult for Jill to negotiate and play cooperatively with her. These reports, coupled with further information about Alice's sister, indicate that your first hypothesis that Jill doesn't want to play baby games in front of her peers was wrong. The correct diagnosis leads to the solution—that is, to help Jill to confront Alice and get her to stop bossing Cindy around.

From this brief example, it is obvious that Alice has to learn that compromise works and that despite age differences, sisters can learn to respect each other's rights and to share. Therefore, if Jill can't get Alice to change, you can talk with Alice about this and intervene appropriately until she understands the concepts and learns the skills she needs for cooperative play. You could also teach Jill some mediation skills. Of course, the more complex problems where you really need to write many anecdotal records will probably not be as simple to diagnose as this. But if you keep good records, the recurring patterns will eventually appear and suggest the solution.

You don't have to write complete accounts of an incident—anecdotal reports can be informal and unstructured. They can include notes, descriptions, or lists of reminders about an event. You can include your reactions and feelings, and you can check the accuracy of observations by asking your children if you are correct.

In observing and interpreting your child's behavior, you can learn to recognize nonverbal communications that signal your child's attitudes, thoughts, and feelings. A simple example is blushing, which usually indicates embarrassment. When your child avoids eye contact with you or someone else, it could be a sign of deception, anger, or even fear. (Of course, you also need to consider the child's background. He or she may be from a culture that teaches children it is disrespectful to look someone in the eye.) So look for the facial expressions and body language that each of your children uses as a way of nonverbal communication and include the information in your records of their behavior.

How Your Behavior Affects Theirs

It is always helpful to determine how your children feel about what you do to encourage good behavior and discourage poor behavior. You don't need any formal way of finding this out—you can simply ask them. You could hold family meetings to determine if your techniques hinder rather than help your relationship with your children.

Donald Dinkmeyer and his colleagues suggest an interesting framework for determining certain typical dimensions of ineffective parenting as perceived by children. If your children believe that you always need to be in control, they may react in an overly dependent or rebellious manner. If they believe that you always act as if you are superior and you are overly dominant or overprotective they may feel stifled in developing independence, responsibility, and self-discipline. If they feel that you always demand reflexive obedience and respect or that you do not show respect or understanding of their feelings and ideas, they may be distrustful of you and all other authority figures.

If you are the type of parent who always insists on parental rights and doesn't recognize that children have rights, you are likely to have kids who will be covertly or overtly resentful and angry. Or they may identify with you and believe that they have more rights than others. If you scored fairly high on the Parent Punitiveness Quiz, you may find that your children perceive you as having many of the negative traits described here. If so, you may realize the folly of punitive parenting.

While you may not be overly punitive, you can cause many problems by being a perfectionist. "So what?" you say. After all, perfectionism is a positive trait in many people. Who would want to go to a physician who was a sloppy thinker or cross a bridge planned by a careless engineer? While perfectionism is an important trait for success, however, it can be maladaptive as a process for parenting. Parenting can not always be governed by mathematical formulas or all the principles of logic, and in the world of parenting and interpersonal relations you can rarely generalize from one cast of characters to another. Just because your oldest child needs very little praise and encouragement to study, that does not mean that your youngest child will be motivated to study without great amounts of praise and encouragement.

The problem with many perfectionist parents is that, even when they try not to, they often communicate feelings of disappointment, impatience, and low regard for children who are not high achievers. So if your children see you as a perfectionist, this could be the cause of a range of problems from underachieving to open rebellion.

Time Sampling of Observable Behaviors

In the section on preventing misbehavior I talked about the importance of catching kids being good. This is based on the behavioral belief that all misbehavior has a function. Most often that function is to gain attention (even negative attention) or to escape from an unpleasant situation. Time sampling can help you to recognize how often you catch your kids being good and praising, reinforcing, or rewarding them and how often you criticize, ridicule, correct in a negative way, threaten punishment, or actually punish them.

Behavioral scientists who study misbehavior use direct observational systems to record behaviors that are both rewarding and punishing. Here is how it works.

After obtaining general background information about a child's behavior, the psychologist and parent or teacher identify the negative "target" behaviors to be observed. Then they identify the positive behaviors they would like to see in place of the negative behaviors. For example, when frustrated, three-year-old Jamie frequently hits her mother. One situation where this behavior occurs is when Jamie demands a cookie before dinner and her mother does not immediately comply. Sometimes Jamie's mother gives in and hands out a cookie, and at other times she smacks Jamie's hand and sends her to her room.

It is desirable that Jamie accept that she can't have the cookie at that time, without trying to retaliate. Therefore when her mother says she can't have the cookie, the desired behavior is for Jamie to stop asking for a cookie or to walk away.

The observer would make a simple tally sheet and count when, where, and how often Jamie hits her mother in that and other situations. The sheet might also include a place for how often her mother praises or rewards Jamie for good behavior. After gathering time samples for a week or so, the results might show that Jamie gets little positive attention from her busy mother. In fact, for every ten times her mother says or does something negative, she praises or catches Jamie being good only one time. It appears that Jamie's request for the cookie is only one in a series of daily bids she makes for attention—any kind of attention—from her mother.

To decrease or end this negative attention-getting behavior, I would advise Jamie's mom to praise her daughter at least ten times a day. At the same time, she should ignore the negative behavior and engage the child in helping her with simple chores as she prepares dinner. That would give her opportunities to praise Jamie for helping set the table and so on. If Jamie asks for a cookie, her mother should tell her in a calm way she can have it later as a reward for being such a good helper.

During this period, the observer would then tally the same behaviors. If the plan worked, the target behavior of hitting would decrease or stop, and the reinforcing statements would increase to at least ten a day.

Now, of course you don't have any trained observers to tally behaviors, so you will have to do it yourself. But you can improvise to make the task easier. For instance, you could leave a Camcorder on for several hours to record what happens, or you could run an audiotape to self-monitor and tally your child's behavior. The important thing is to get some sense of how your responses to your child's misbehavior may actually be driving that unwanted behavior.

Give Appropriate Feedback to Your Child

Once you have some idea about what goes on between you and your child, you can begin to use some very basic and extremely effective techniques of communication. These are techniques used by most mental health professionals to demonstrate empathy, concern, and understanding to their clients. You can and should use these with your child to prevent and deal with misbehavior. They all fall under the rubric of feedback.

Accept Your Child's Feelings as Genuine

When seven-year-old Billy messes up his older brother Jimmy's Super Nintendo, Jimmy starts screaming and calling him every curse word that can possibly exist in the vocabulary of a ten-year-old. Should you smack Jimmy, wash his mouth out with soap, or send him to his room? Before you do any of the above, think.

Jimmy really enjoys his Super Nintendo. Billy knows that he is not supposed to play with it unless he gets permission from Jimmy because Billy has his own Sega system. Not only does Billy play with the Super Nintendo when Jimmy is not around, he damages Aladdin, one of Jimmy's favorite video games. Now, doesn't Jimmy have good reason to be mad? You betcha!

Jimmy's feelings are genuine and appropriate. But is the way he expresses his feelings appropriate for the setting? The answer is no, because he knows that you will not accept cursing in the house. So what do you do?

Here is the first thing you should say: "Jimmy, I know you are angry at your brother for taking your toys, but I will not allow you to call him names. You can tell him how upset you are that he messed up your Aladdin game, and you have a right to ask him to make good for what he did. Do you want him to use his allowance to get you a new Aladdin game, or do you have a different idea?"

Your actions have let him know you accept his anger as genuine and justified. You have shown respect for his ability to negotiate a solution to the problem. You have also reinforced your firmness about not allowing cursing. But rather than losing it about the cursing, you are teaching him how to deal with his anger appropriately. If you lose it and scream, smack him, or send him to his room, what has he learned from the incident? He has learned—from your model—that when you get angry, it is OK to hurt and insult the offender. But if Jimmy persists in cursing after you give him other options, then you can move on to consider punishment. This is a very different matter from starting with a punitive approach.

Children must learn that at times we all have feelings that are not nice. Sometimes we can not help feeling angry, hostile, or vengeful. But we learn not to act on those feelings when the results of those actions are harmful to others. This is quite different from trying to make a child feel guilt and remorse for having feelings that are unacceptable to parents. It is important to regularly model expressions of feelings, especially positive ones such as warmth, love, and concern. Also, acceptance and encouragement of expressions of feelings by everyone in the home facilitates children's understanding of the universality of feelings and the concept that it is good to share them with others.

It is always more difficult to communicate with a child during stressful situations, so it is best to learn to reflect feelings during normal types of situations. By using reflective or active listening, you indicate that you really understand your child's feelings, and you enhance the possibility for two-way communication. The idea is that you are a mirror that accurately reflects back the child's feelings. The only way that you will know if you are accurate is to get feedback from the child. You can practice by trying to recognize various feelings such as sadness, remorse, puzzlement, and happiness.

The basic procedure begins by stating what you think is the child's feeling. If you are wrong, you will be corrected, unless the child is afraid to reveal true feelings to you. If this is the case, you need to think about why your child can't be honest with you. Next, convey understanding by saying something like, "I know how you feel, and you have a right to feel that way."

Your children should come to believe that they will not be embarrassed, humiliated, or punished for showing or expressing their feelings. However, you must also indicate that although you accept their feelings, this does not mean that you will approve or accept inappropriate expressions of these feelings. Even though you can demonstrate or model empathy and respect for children's feelings and you can demonstrate that you understand them, you are still the parent and you can limit the way those feelings are expressed if they hurt someone else.

Accept Your Child's Ideas as Authentic

Thirteen-year-old Jeff comes home after the first month of science classes. Rather than his usual routine of saying hello and going to the refrigerator for a snack, Jeff throws his book bag on the floor, drops his jacket on a couch, and heads for the family room where he immediately turns on MTV. When you ask what's wrong, without taking his eyes of the TV, he says he hates Mr. Rand, his science teacher.

If you're in this situation, you may or may not have to turn off the TV, but you need to get Jeff to focus on you and to convey to him that you are willing to listen to his ideas about why he hates Mr. Rand. You may already know why. For instance, you may have information that Mr. Rand is a poor teacher—or that he is a good teacher and Jeff is a poor student in science. But you should not prejudge or express your own opinions about the matter until you know what Jeff thinks.

As in accepting feelings, it is important to demonstrate your understanding of Jeff's ideas and your acceptance that even though they may be incorrect, he has a right to express them. He should never be embarrassed, humiliated, or punished for saying what he thinks. They are his ideas, and until he gets them out and explores them fully, they are authentic and unchangeable. It is important to help him, in a nonjudgmental way, to explore his ideas by summarizing, clarifying, restating and extending them. Here is an example:

PARENT: So you really hate Mr. Rand. (*Accurately reflecting Jeff's feelings.*)

JEFF: Yes, I want to get out of his class.

PARENT: You want to get out of his class? (*Accurately reflecting Jeff's idea.*) What has happened?

JEFF: Mr. Rand is always putting kids down. He ridicules us if we don't have the answers he wants. I can't stand him.

PARENT: So you think he bullies kids? *(Restating what Jeff said, without questioning or judging him.)*

JEFF: Yeah! Today we had a lab period. My experiment didn't come out exactly right, and he accused me of not paying attention to the instructions and of being too interested in staring at Jenny.

PARENT: So he really embarrassed you. *(Reflecting a probable feeling.)* Tell me exactly what happened. *(Soliciting detailed information.)*

After all the details are clear, you can summarize the situation and then begin to explore the options. It may be that Mr. Rand is abusive to students, but there may not be any other science classes available, so Jeff is stuck for the duration. You and Jeff may decide that one option is to confront Mr. Rand about his behavior and determine his perception of how he deals with his students. It is possible that Mr. Rand is just joking and needs feedback from parents about how he is perceived by the students. It is possible that Jeff has not been doing his assignments and has been fooling around in class. You may talk to other parents to see if their children are having the same types of problems with Mr. Rand. If so, you may want to organize the parents to talk to the principal.

The major point of all this is that Jeff feels that his parent listens to his complaints, respects his right to express himself, and helps him to decide on his options. You can make it clear that accepting Jeff's ideas does not indicate that you approve or accept his plans to misbehave based on those ideas. For instance, if the evidence indicates that Mr. Rand is unfair and that attempts to make him change don't work, Jeff is likely to decide that he will not work hard in the class or that he will get revenge by playing some practical jokes on Mr. Rand.

If Jeff's plans are potentially self-destructive, you must make him think of the various consequences. You might say, "I understand that you think Mr. Rand is mean, sarcastic, and unfair, but you are stuck with him. Let's look at what the consequences are for what you want to do." Without making judgments, demands, or interpretations that are demeaning, you must encourage and allow Jeff to express either agreement or disagreement with your ideas. Going through problem solving together with you will help Jeff to appraise his own thinking and increase his verbal skills and monitor the practicality of his thinking.

By giving Jeff the opportunity to express his own opinions, you will help foster in him a sense of ownership, independence, and power in terms of his ability to solve problems. You are helping him to develop problem-solving skills and critical thinking. Parents should not be judgmental and put down the child's perception of the problem. The key is to help the child develop realistic solutions, even if initial perceptions of the cause may be incorrect.

If you say to Jeff, "You want to get out of his class," you have accurately reflected his idea. You might also restate his idea and add an interpretation in a way that shows you understand what he is thinking and that opens the way to further exploration. This procedure involves insight and real understanding. For instance you could say, "So, you want to get out of Mr. Rand's class so you can look forward to going to school again." If this is correct, Jeff will agree and probably pick up on the theme that he really hates going to school because of Mr. Rand. If it is wrong, he will probably say something like, "No, that's not it—I know I will always have some bad teachers, and I won't let them spoil my life."

Give Children Verbal Feedback About Their Behavior

Your ten-year-old son, Gary, has begun to tease his twelve-year-old sister, Jessica, who has begun to develop breasts and has recently shown an interest in boys. One day, while they are watching television, a romantic scene appears on the screen. As they are watching it Gary starts in: "Oh, Oh, Jess, look they are playing kissy face. Is that how you do it with that creep Jim?"

As expected, Jessica responds angrily, "Shut up, you dork. You don't have to worry about kissing, because no girl in her right mind would ever kiss you!"

Now that Gary has provoked Jessica to say something mean, he feels justified in escalating the argument. He goes for the jugular. "Yeah, well, the only reason Jim kisses you is because he wants to grab those little boobs of yours."

Jessica, who is very sensitive about her developing body, begins to cry. She counterattacks: "You little sleaze, one more word and I will smack that filthy little mouth of yours."

As the dispute becomes louder, you enter the scene and ask what happened. You get a fairly accurate replay of the events and realize that Gary started by teasing his sister. Which of the following actions should you take?

1. Let them fight it out.
2. Tell them both that you don't want to hear that kind of talk and punish both for name calling.
3. Find out why Gary started with Jessica, tell them what they did wrong, and explore with them what each could have done instead.
4. Wash out Gary's mouth with soapy water for being obscene with his sister.
5. Smack Gary and send him to his room.

Action 1, ignoring the situation, isn't going to have any real impact on the siblings' behavior—and neither will actions 2, 4, and 5. It is obvious from this brief scenario that the hostility and jealousy between Gary and Jessica has simmered and exploded before. But action 3 offers the beginning of a solution. The focus is on providing objective feedback about the misbehavior and a description of appropriate behavior. This technique facilitates communication of parental expectations, the setting of limits, and praise and approval for appropriate behavior. The attempt is to discourage rather than punish misbehavior. You should describe the unacceptable behavior, state acceptable behavior for each situation and then discuss alternative ways of handling the feelings underlying the misbehavior. In this case you could say, "Gary, I have listened to both of you and this is my understanding of what happened. You were both watching this show when a kissing scene came on, and you began to tease your sister. Jess, you then called him names and put him down. He came back at you, and it sounded to me like you were about to hit him. Now, I do not like what happened because you were nasty to each other. Gary, I know you can be mature and responsible. The next time a kissing scene comes on, you can comment on it as long as you don't make dirty comments to your sister or relate her in any way to the television show. However, if you insist on doing that, you are telling me you want to be punished. This can be arranged."

This statement gives Gary feedback about his behavior and lets him know it is unacceptable and that there are limits. However, it does not immediately threaten Gary with draconian punishments; it leaves the consequences up to Gary's imagination. It also tells him what behavior is expected in similar situations. You next turn to Jessica and say, "Now, Jessica, you know what will happen if you let Gary's teasing bother you. You get upset easily and react exactly how Gary knows you will. You put him down, and then he has an excuse to get back at you. The next time this happens, I want you to ignore it. If you can't, then get up and leave. I know you shouldn't have to stop watching a show because of what Gary says, but you can watch it in your room. If this happens several times, let me know about it. But I know that you are mature enough to handle this in a grown-up way."

This statement tells Jessica what she did and what she should do instead. It recognizes how easily she can get upset but also describes the reaction as not accomplishing anything positive. It gives her an appropriate strategy to use when being teased. It also assures her that if the strategy does not work, you would be avail-able to support her.

In this very touchy situation you have tried to provide feedback in an objective, nondemeaning way. You let both children know what you expect of them and what you will and will not accept. You included praise and encouragement for good behaviors as well as discussion of inappropriate behaviors. As part of giving feedback, you offered help in coming up with solutions. You saw this as an opportunity to work on solutions to the problems between the sib-lings rather than as a situation requiring punishment.

Derogatory, demeaning, and generally negative responses to misbehavior put the child on the spot, draw attention to the mis-behavior, and set the stage for a power struggle. Verbal abuse, including angry screaming and shouting and sarcastic putdowns, is counterproductive—it causes resentment, anger, loss of face, and the desire to retaliate.

Verbal feedback should always be clear and firm. You should look directly at the child and use his or her name. You may even touch or gently hold the child while making your point. If your children refuse to comply, refuse to take responsibility for their own behavior, or respond inappropriately to your demands, you can use the broken record technique, as explained by Thomas Gordon. In the *broken record technique*, you state what you want from the child with a preface such as "This is what I want you to do." Avoid get-ting diverted from your goal by firmly repeating your request a max-imum of three times. If there is no adequate response, be prepared to follow through with a consequence. For example,

PARENT: I want you to stop teasing your brother.

CHILD: But I didn't mean to.

PARENT: That's not the point, I want you to stop teasing your brother!

CHILD: But I didn't mean to.

PARENT: I understand what you said, but I want you to stop teasing your brother.

CHILD: OK, but he better leave me alone.

PARENT: If you tease him again, you will go to time-out.

Now, you may ask how this is different from nagging. It is different because (1) you are very focused on the message, (2) you will only do it three times, and (3) you clearly state consequences that you are fully prepared to execute.

When providing feedback about misbehavior, you may also relate other situations when the child exhibited similar misbehaviors. You must be careful when doing this because the message is not to "prove" to children how bad they are. Rather, the goal is to help children see their misbehavior as others see it, to understand their misbehavior, and to realize how their actions affect others. You can also include *I-messages*—a concept that I believe was first introduced by Hiam Ginott and later expanded by Thomas Gordon. This is a three-part verbal technique using a nonblameful, nonevaluative message that communicates how you feel or experience the child's misbehavior. You describe the misbehavior, tell about the effect it has on you, and indicate your feelings about it. Instead of making a denigrating comment such as "Bill, you are a disgusting pig when that kind of dirty language comes out of your mouth," you would say, "I really feel upset, embarrassed, and ashamed when I hear my son talk like that." Instead of putting Bill down and telling him how disgusting he is, in this case you let him know how you feel—and throw in a little old-fashioned guilt for good measure.

Discuss Your Children's Negative Behavior with Them

The best time to discuss children's negative behavior is when they are good. The purpose is to find out the reasons why the child misbehaved and to discuss alternatives. Of course this technique is not all that useful with younger children, who may not remember the misbehavior or may be afraid you are bringing it up to punish them. Also, of course, this is not something that should be done frequently, because then children may begin to feel that the only time you want to talk with them is when you talk about their faults.

Modify the Ecology

I use *ecology* here to refer to the physical systems and logistical factors that influence a child's life. The ecological factors that affect the functioning of human families are, in broad terms, no different than those that affect endangered species such as the spotted owl. Successful survival depends on the control and use of such internal aspects of their environment as space, recreation, shelter, communication, and privacy. Survival is also dependent on ability to maneuver in and control external systems such as schools and workplaces and the availability of resources.

Physical Ecology

The physical ecology for a child includes, but is not limited to, the child's room, the layout of the house, toys, school materials, sports equipment, clothes, food, automobiles (if the youth drives), the immediate outside environment that forms the boundaries of the child's independent travels, the places the child normally travels to by car or bus such as school, places of worship, and homes of friends and relatives. Each of these can be used in ways that provide for a child's development, education, entertainment, and punishment. For instance, a new Nintendo game can give a child great pleasure, but restricting the amount of time it can be used provides a punishment.

Systems

Systems consist of groups of people who function together within a set of formal and informal rules or agreements. Organizations such as families, schools, businesses, and the military are all systems. In this book we are mainly interested in family systems. Each family has its own operating system that is made up of stated and unstated rules, assumptions, and practices. These systems may subvert or maintain good behavior. For instance, many practitioners of systems approaches to family therapy claim that misbehavior may be the child's attempt to divert attention from other family problems. The classic case is the child whose unconscious motivation to misbehave is to divert parents from fighting with each other constantly about other issues, such as finances, which might lead to divorce.

When boundaries in the system are not clear, misbehavior may occur. For instance, while grandparents may overindulge or establish rules for children in their own home, they are not the parents and should not interfere with the way the children are raised. In my practice I have helped many parents who survived very punitive and often abusive homes and are trying to raise their own children differently. When these parents have children with problems, their own parents often encourage spanking as the main solution to the problem. Punitive grandparents are sometimes part of the situation that brings clients to me.

The most frustrating aspect of dealing with grandparents who were abusive as parents is that they invariably deny the abuse they inflicted on their own children. They claim that they used "normal" spanking. Meanwhile, their grown children, who are now trying to discover nonpunitive ways of dealing with behavior problems, only want their parents to apologize and admit they were wrong. That type of confession is rarely forthcoming and therefore it is not possible to have clear boundary lines between grandparents, parents, and grandchildren in regard to discipline. All parties feel that the others are incompetent to raise the children and that they themselves must therefore cross the lines to intervene on behalf of the children. Children can use this confusion to manipulate all parties.

These grandparents are often very disturbed when their grown children seek help outside the family. They frequently try to discourage or sabotage the parental alliance with a psychologist by undermining credence in psychology and psychologists, thereby further trying to confuse boundaries.

Logistics

Logistics refers to schedules, movement from place to place, and arrangements. In the frantic family life of the 1990s, few parents underestimate the importance of balancing work and family responsibilities. The need for orderly, efficient transition from one activity to another is a constant source of frustration for many parents. This puts tremendous strain on parents who have problems themselves with impulse control and temper.

For example, getting children ready for school can become a big problem when both parents work. When parents must follow a fixed schedule in the morning, an oppositional child can wreak havoc by going back to sleep, dawdling, or feigning illness. I usually interpret this as a power struggle between child and parent—and one that children can almost always win if parents don't outsmart them with good planning.

Good logistical planning is much more effective than spanking, screaming, and nagging. Such planning includes consequences, both positive for the child being ready on time, and negative for not being ready. It includes simple solutions such as making lunch the night before and laying out clothes for the next morning, using a timer with a loud signal to indicate where a child should be at each stage of preparation, and actually planning to go through the entire procedure with the child every day. More complicated logistical planning may include having an older sibling help, arranging for backup to take over if you anticipate running too late, or even hiring someone to come in each morning for a few hours to help. There are many retired people who would love such a job. Also, you may have to accept that your child may miss school or be late, but will face consequences each time this happens.

Ecological approaches to discipline emphasize that children need to understand that parents must maintain limits and enforce reasonable rules. When children are in charge, they prevent parents from doing their job, and everyone suffers in the long run. Some children who are in charge develop a warped sense of how the world works, although some understand boundaries and only manipulate them at home where they are successful. They don't behave in this manner in school and other settings where they know their manipulations won't work.

Character development is in many ways dependent on how the ecology is used. For instance, teaching a preschool child to share favorite toys with others or encouraging a seventeen-year-old to contribute time each week for driving senior citizens to the hospital or shopping help both to develop a sense of responsibility. In the same manner irresponsibility may be encouraged by overindulging a child's appetites for material goods or allowing a child to destroy toys without any consequences. Consider the case of Kevin.

Kevin the Destroyer

Mrs. Leary came to me with five-year-old Kevin, who was completely out of control. She complained that he insisted on getting every toy advertised on TV. If he didn't get what he wanted he cried, whined, and nagged until she gave in. He got bored with most toys after several weeks and was just as likely to destroy them as to ignore them. She was unable to get him to pick them up, so toys were strewn all over the house.

Kevin generally did not whine to his father. Mr. Leary was very active in his business and often came home late or brought work home on weekends. Nonetheless, he was a loving father and devoted husband and felt guilty that he didn't spend more time with Kevin. He left most of the disciplining to his wife and supported her when she asked for help.

It was clear from other problems we discussed that Mrs. Leary had her own problems in being assertive. One of her problems was that she believed that giving her son everything he wanted would ensure his continuing love. She grew up in a poor working-class family where the seven siblings had few toys. As a child she was frequently spanked by an alcoholic father and an ill-tempered, frustrated, unhappy mother who periodically flew into rages.

Mrs. Leary, who was always a good student, was able to overcome her family's destructive impact. She earned an MBA, and when I saw her she had a very well paying job in a bank as a senior financial analyst. She and her husband, who was a corporate executive, lived the good life. With her vastly improved economic situation and her high level of education, she vowed to provide her son with all she could and swore to never hit him. Now that part is OK, but she didn't have a clue as to how to set limits. She just never learned as a child that loving parents can set limits and make children follow reasonable rules without the use of physical force.

While we worked on Mrs. Leary's fear of rejection by her son if she didn't give him everything he wanted, we discussed how she could set clear limits. She understood that her son was clearly in control of the home environment. We developed a written set of rules and I worked with her each week to implement them in a fair but firm way. These rules were:

- All toys must be kept in the playroom or bedroom. Any toys found in other places would be confiscated for two days.
- Before bedtime every day, Kevin, with his mother's help if required, would put all toys in the bedroom and playroom on the shelves or in the toy chest. (The Learys installed ample storage space as part of the plan.)
- Kevin would be limited to one new toy a month, except for special occasions.
- Any toys that Kevin did not want were to be given to a day-care center for poor children, although he could keep toys as long as he desired if they were stored properly.
- If Kevin broke any toys on purpose he would lose his newest toy for three days. Because five-year-olds don't have a good sense of time, a calendar was used to check off punishment

days when toys were removed so he would know when they would be returned.

Mrs. Leary needed support to ignore Kevin's nagging and whining during the first month. She developed clear boundaries between Kevin and herself. He began to realize she was in charge, not him. She also arranged the logistics of the situation by setting a time when toys had to be put away. Change was not immediate, but with several months of calm, consistent rule enforcement, Kevin's behavior became developmentally appropriate.

Modifications in the physical ecology of the home don't require a sophisticated understanding of psychological theory. In fact, they are often so simple that parents may not think of them. Let me give you one more example that represents one of the most common problems I encounter with oppositional kids at around age twelve or thirteen. I used to call this the pigsty syndrome, but in keeping with contemporary adolescent vernacular I now call it the grunge syndrome.

The Grunge Syndrome

Mr. and Mrs. Phillips came to me because their fourteen-year-old son, Bryon, was doing poorly in school. But as they started to list Bryon's many techniques of resisting authority and parental requests, Mrs. Phillips became most agitated as she described what a complete slob her son was. Here is the sad tale.

From the time Bryon got up in the morning, he left a trail of chaos and carnage behind him. His pajamas sprawled on the floor, wet towels on his bed finished off a watery trail from his private bathroom following his morning shower, toothpaste was invariably left open, and the hair in his drain was beginning to look like the results of a visit from the Addams family's cousin It.

When Bryon came home from school, the evidence of his arrival included his jacket on the floor near the front door, an open and partially filled milk container and other remnants of his snack on the kitchen counter, footgear of the day strategically left in the family room so that someone invariably tripped over it, and socks, shoes, and clothes cast asunder in his bedroom. Despite pleas, demands, and punishments, especially from his mother (who admitted she was a clean freak), this scenario had continued during the past year. The steady state of filth was only interrupted briefly as the result of draconian punishments. In addition to this ongoing battle, a humongous amount of parental energy was consumed in trying to deal with Bryon's poor grades and avoidance of homework.

Mrs. Phillips complained bitterly that after working all day she had to spend the first half hour or more picking up after Bryon. She just couldn't start dinner thinking about how filthy the house was.

During the initial family session, Bryon sat passively, sometimes smirking and sometimes obviously daydreaming. When I asked him if all this was true, he said that his mother exaggerated. When his father corroborated the description, Bryon said, "What do you think Dad would say. He has to agree with Mom. He is afraid to drop a sock on the floor because he knows Mom will wipe him out. We all know that she is in charge. Dad is just a wuss."

I saw this immediately as the old ploy of divide and conquer. Divert the issue from his sloppiness to which parent was dominant. I didn't fall for it. I went on to ask Bryon about his personal cleanliness. He replied that he took at least a twenty-minute shower every morning. This included the use of generous amounts of shampoo and conditioner and was followed by his special technique of blow drying his hair. I commented that he did not appear to be a slob, because he was well groomed and was wearing clean, trendy clothes. He said he changed all his clothes each day and had a great wardrobe. He also used a deodorant and brushed and flossed his teeth at least twice a day. He hardly seemed like the type to be happy in a pigsty. But he sure knew how to push all of his mother's buttons.

I won't go into all of the treatment that was needed to help Bryon and his parents realize that much of his behavior was driven by anger at his high-achieving perfectionist mother. But let me tell you the ecological changes that were made to solve the problem of his clothes and his bathroom. Here is the dialogue between me and his mother.

ME: Mrs. Phillips, it is clear to me that Bryon has good personal hygiene. In fact, he seems in some ways to be what he accuses you of. He is somewhat of a clean freak himself. What I don't understand is how he keeps his clothes so well.

MRS. PHILLIPS: Can't you guess? Of course, I am the one who picks up all his clothes. He thinks I am his slave. I am the one who washes, dries, and folds them. I am the one who takes everything to the cleaner.

ME: But I don't understand. When you know that he is not personally a slob, why do you do all those things for him? Why don't you just leave his clothes on the floor until he picks them up and washes them himself?

MRS. PHILLIPS: Are you kidding? I couldn't live in such a mess. Besides, what would people think of me if they saw the house like that? I would be totally embarrassed.

ME: But you aren't the slob. Your son is. Besides, he is not really a slob—he is meticulous about his personal cleanliness. I call this a variation of the grunge syndrome. While he acts like a slob at home, he knows that dirty clothes and smelly bodies are really not cool among his peers. You can use that to gain control.

MRS. PHILLIPS: What do you mean? I have tried everything, and believe me, nothing works.

ME: Well, there is a basic plan, with several variations, that I have found is usually successful in these situations. But you have a choice. Do you want to go on living like this or are you willing take a short-term gamble at the price of maybe being embarrassed?

MRS. PHILLIPS: What are you suggesting?

ME: Well, from what I know about this situation, I think that Bryon is trying to make a point with you—and he is winning.

MRS. PHILLIPS: Oh, I know that he enjoys driving me mad. So what's new?

ME: What's new is that you are not going to let him win. You can do this by what I call simple ecological manipulation based on the fact that Bryon is controlling what you do with his clothes, his bathroom, the kitchen, and so on. Basically, you are going to tell him that from now on, since he wants to be in control, he can have *full* control. Let's first deal with his clothes, which is the simplest problem to solve. But for you, it will not be easy at first.

The basic idea is that from now on, at some level, you will have nothing to do with his clothes unless he follows your rules. In other words, you will leave them any place they are left, you will never wash them or take them to the dry cleaner, and—since he can't follow the rules—only in extremely rare circumstances will you buy him any new clothes.

MRS. PHILLIPS: You have got to be kidding. After a week or two we couldn't get past the front door. The living room and family room would be jammed full. Besides, his room would start to stink from his dirty clothes lying around, not to mention what the wet towels would do to the bed.

ME: You are right, but eventually he will run out of clean clothes. Then what? Do you really think he will go to school or on dates in dirty underwear or socks?

MRS. PHILLIPS: I guess you are right, but I don't know if I can deal with this.

ME: Well, there are other variations on this basic ecological maneuver. For instance, you could refuse to wash any clothes that are not in the hamper, you could insist that he wash his own clothes, or you could confiscate and hide any clothes that are not where they should be. It is up to you. You could start with the toughest program or try one you find easier at first. But the basic deal is that he must learn that he can't infringe on your rights to keep a clean house.

After thinking about what to do and discussing it with her husband, who said he would support her, Mrs. Phillips decided to go whole hog. We had a family therapy session, and Bryon laughed at the whole thing. He stated that his mom was incapable of leaving clothes on the floor more than two seconds after she saw them. The battle was on.

With help from me and support from her husband, Mrs. Phillips stuck to the plan. For the first week, Bryon tested her in every way possible. He bragged to friends that he was the king of grunge and that it was really funny to watch his mother as she resisted picking things up. But as the second and third week rolled around and Bryon began to run out of clean clothes and his room smelled like his armpit after several hours of basketball, it wasn't so funny. Finally, he asked for a truce.

At a family therapy session, Bryon and his parents made a written contract to improve his slovenly behavior. This included things other than his clothes. His mother agreed to wash all clothes that made it to the hamper every Saturday morning by nine o'clock, which was her regular wash time. Any clothes not in the hamper must be washed by Bryon himself. However, any dirty clothes left lying around in plain sight by seven o'clock each evening would be confiscated and placed in a locked box for three weeks.

In order to add a positive approach, we set it up so that if Bryon washed everyone's clothes on Wednesdays to help his stressed parents, he could earn credit toward the eventual purchase of a car, which he wanted very badly. After hearing about a car, Bryon then suggested other chores he could do toward its purchase. The family continued to work on other issues, but the grunge syndrome, with a few minor relapses, was cured. See if you can identify the physical, systems, and logistical aspects of the plan that we used.

Other Aspects of Ecological Systems Management

Good, ecologically based discipline requires planning. Here are some aspects of this, although this list is far from exhaustive:

- *Provide an adequate number and variety of developmentally appropriate structured activities for your children.* These range from activity boards that ring, bang, and play recorded voices and sounds for infants to board games for older children to scouting and sports for preteens and adolescents.

- *Always use objects of interest to distract toddlers who want to do something wrong.* This works much better than spanking and is usually quite simple.

- *When necessary, negotiate family rules with your kids, then post the rules.* Rules should be specific, clearly defined, and stated in behavioral terms that describe what to do rather than what not to do. For instance, use, "When mom and dad are talking, wait until the person speaking is done before you say anything," rather than, "Don't interrupt others when they are talking." Another example is to use, "When you get angry with your brother, use words to tell him how you feel and try to compromise to resolve your disagreement," rather than, "Do not fight with your brother."

Children should be allowed to suggest rules of reasonable conduct for parents. For instance they might suggest that you should not nag, scream, or yell if they don't immediately comply with a parental request. Successful rules are more likely if children and parents initially negotiate them and are able to later change them with mutual consent.

You should have as few rules as possible. They should be simple, easy to memorize, and developmentally appropriate. When setting up rules, be democratic and reasonable, but remember that you weren't elected and you are the parents, so you do have the final say when issues such as safety and health are involved.

- *Plan for effective prevention of misbehavior.* Allow adequate time, recognize constraints, and take into account each child's developmental level, maturity, and attention span. In the process provide for adequate physical facilities (such as a quiet place to do homework), and provide for varying patterns of family interaction (opportunity for parents to spend quality time alone with each child, time for whole family activities, and time for parent-only activities).

• *Be prepared to use physical restraint if needed.* The purpose of physical restraint is to deter children from hurting themselves or others or destroying property—without hurting the child. Restraint techniques in institutional settings require intensive training. As in those settings, they should be used only when absolutely necessary. I describe these techniques in detail in Chapter Seven, when I discuss anger and resentment.

A major argument of those in favor of spanking is that you must smack toddlers to discourage them from harming themselves or property. Images of toddlers running into the street, drinking Drano, swallowing bottles of aspirin, or breaking valuable objects are invoked. The ecological answer is to physically control the environment so toddlers don't have an opportunity cause harm. You can buy childproofing kits that provide covers for electrical sockets and hooks for cabinet doors and drawers. Put valuable objects such as porcelain out of their reach. Eliminate tablecloths, doilies, and other coverings until your toddler is old enough to know not to pull on them.

In this chapter I have laid the groundwork for preventing misbehavior and effectively disciplining children. To accomplish these goals you must diagnose the causes of unacceptable behavior. I have suggested some techniques for doing this, and I have also given you some ideas about how to communicate with your children after misbehaviors occur. I have also stressed the importance of ecological factors in preventing and dealing with problems.

Although I accept the need for punishment, other than corporal punishment or verbal abuse, here I have shown you nonpunitive, rational ways to prevent and control situations that can easily escalate into repeated cycles of misbehavior and punishment. In the next chapter, I tell you how to use punishment if it becomes necessary.

6

Rewards and Punishments

When Dolores Lally and I conducted a study of discipline training programs in 1984, the influence of behaviorism was much less noticeable than it is today. Now, almost all discipline training programs address the issues of reward and punishment, although they don't all agree on how they should be used. But while language and conceptualizations differ, everyone agrees that children need to feel good about themselves and benefit from both *extrinsic* (external) and *intrinsic* (internal) systems of reward and motivation.

In the first part of this chapter I discuss the concepts of reward and punishment that constitute the core of behavioral approaches to discipline. These techniques involve the use of extrinsic reinforcers—specific rewards such as money, good grades, treats, and praise that are generally administered by parents and teachers in an effort to motivate children to change their behavior. In the second part I will discuss intrinsic systems of reward based on humanistic and democratic ideals. These are based on the belief that when children learn appropriate behavior through discussion, their inborn motivations for empathy, caring, concern, and competence will emerge as they become "good" children.

The External-Internal Debate

One of my neighbors read a draft of this book and liked much of it—but was appalled by the idea of systematically rewarding children with money as a way to improve their behavior. Now, she is a very caring, gentle, educated mother who has never hit her two young well-behaved daughters. But she is typical of many parents and teachers who, even if they understand the scientific basis for the use of external rewards, would never use certain types of rewards to get a child to comply. Their reaction reflects an ongoing debate among discipline experts about external versus internal techniques to motivate children to behave.

Behavioral scientists would say that both praise and money are external motivators or reinforcers. I will talk about the specifics of these a little later, but it is important for you to consider what I say in as objective a way as possible.

The debate about the relative merits of external and internal reinforcers will probably never lead to a consensus. The two sides are driven by philosophical assumptions about the nature of people and how a society should operate. I do agree with humanists and Adlerians that it is best when children are internally motivated. I also see no problem with using external reinforcers when necessary. Further, a recent major synthesis of the research shows that the use of external rewards does not interfere with children's internal motivations. Personally, I think you should use all sorts of rewards.

Many are aghast at the idea of giving children rewards such as money to do what they should already be doing. They tend to call it bribery. But that word should really be reserved for rewards given in exchange for illegal or unethical acts. When I suggest the use of money or some other external reinforcer to some parents, they complain that it is bribery until I help them see the role of external rewards in their own lives. Every employed individual is rewarded by money. In the best of all possible worlds, the harder you work, the more monetary rewards you receive. You don't see many corporate CEOs turning down mega salaries, stock options, and promises of golden parachutes just for the joy of helping the corporation. So why is it that we tend to believe that children should be good, just because they should be good?

Contrary to what I have just said, if you take a parenting course based on the theories of Alfred Adler, you will be told that external rewards such as praise, money, or gifts should not be used to obtain compliance from children or to motivate them. Adlerians such as Donald Dinkmeyer feel that praise is patronizing and manipulative. They claim that praise is judgmental. For instance, if Johnny comes home with an A and you praise him or give him a reward, he will feel that your praise is dependent upon him earning A's. If he earns a B the next time, and you don't praise him, he will assume that you are being critical and you are devaluing him.

Donald Dinkmeyer distinguishes between praise and encouragement. Rather than externally motivating children, encouragement stimulates the development of internal motivation. Adlerians believe that encouragement recognizes effort and improvement and includes a respectful and appreciative attitude toward children. Encouragement tells your children that they are good enough just the way they are, and separates what they do from who they are. Encouragement teaches them that mistakes are not something to be ashamed of but are opportunities to grow and learn, thus enhancing the child's self-esteem. For instance, when Johnny brings home an A, instead of praising him for the A, mom uses encouragement by saying, "How do you feel about earning an A? If earning an A makes you feel good, then that's what you should do. I love you whether you earn an A or a B. When you are proud of your grades, then I am happy for you."

Well, there you have it. The two views about rewards. You can choose either, but I recommend using the best of both sets of beliefs. Let's begin with a brief explanation of the behavioral approach to using rewards and punishment. We will then discuss the alternate view, based on humanistic beliefs.

How Extrinsic Rewards and Punishments Work

Early in this book I promised you I wouldn't use any psychobabble. However, since so much of discipline is related to reward and punishment, this section deserves a technical discussion. I want you to learn the scientific meanings of some terms that will help you to use some of the most powerful yet controversial concepts devised to influence human behavior. The science of behavioral psychology is based on the assumption, backed by extensive research, that all behavior is driven by reward and punishment. Further, despite so-called commonsense beliefs in the effectiveness of punishments, the overwhelming evidence indicates that rewards or reinforcements (I use these terms interchangeably) are the most powerful shapers and changers of behavior.

Now you may scoff at the idea that you should use rewards to get ten-year-old Craig to stop lying, to motivate seven-year-old Jenny who has Attention-Deficit Hyperactivity Disorder, or to stop seventeen-year-old Paul from smoking marijuana. You may scoff, but you don't know what trainers of wild animals such as lions, tigers, elephants, and porpoises know. Try spanking a lion or an elephant and see where it gets you! As animal trainers and behaviorists know, animals and people respond to rewards and punishments in similar manners.

Behaviorists have demonstrated across species that rewards can be used in systematic ways to shape desired behaviors. In difficult situations various types of punishments may have to be used in combination with rewards, but it is clear that punishment generally has only short-term effectiveness. Regular parental dependence on punishment has too many negative side effects. We will discuss these a little later.

One of the technical terms I am going the throw at you in order to help you to use behavioral techniques is *contingency management*. This refers to the use of rewards and punishments to fit each contingency or situation.

In the past I have used the following table (Table 6.1) to help teachers understand the basics of using rewards and punishments. You will notice that there are three types of punishments, but no mention of corporal punishment. In the over sixty years of behavioral research on reward and punishment that I have reviewed, I have found only a few studies that suggest the use of corporal punishment in normal parenting situations, and I believe that these studies were flawed. Now, asking you to remember that we are only discussing punishment that is not physically painful or psychologically demeaning (excessive criticism, sarcasm, name calling, put-downs, yelling, and so on), I will define and discuss examples of the proper use of reward and punishment.

You will notice that at the top of the table, the headings indicate how to *increase* the possibility of good behavior or *decrease* the possibility of misbehavior. To deal with these two dimensions, you can either *give* or *remove* something, as indicated on the left margin of the table. For instance, good behaviors are increased by giving rewards (positive reinforcement) or removing aversive conditions (negative reinforcement). Misbehaviors are decreased by giving discomfort until the misbehavior stops (punishment) or removing the child from a rewarding, pleasant, or comfortable situation until the child agrees to behave (deprivation punishment).

TABLE 6.1 How Punishment and Reward Work.

	Increase Good Behaviors by Using	*Decrease Misbehaviors by Using*
G I V E	POSITIVE REINFORCEMENT such as praise, money, stars, privileges	PUNISHMENT such as verbal reprimands, unpleasant consequences, withdrawal of privileges
R E M O V E	NEGATIVE REINFORCEMENT such as stopping or removing unpleasant or aversive conditions	DEPRIVATION PUNISHMENT such as time out from play, family activities, television, and so on

Rewarding

There are two kinds of reward systems: positive reinforcement and negative reinforcement. Both operate according to the belief that if what you do gets reinforced, you will be likelier to do whatever it is again.

Positive Reinforcement

A positive reinforcement or reward is something you say, do, or give to a child following a particular behavior. Your goal should always be to "catch kids being good." Here is an example of how this type of reward technique might play out.

Three-year-old Timmy is playing quietly, sorting different shapes. You say, "You are playing so nicely, Timmy. I like to see you play with those toys." This is a simple but effective way to encourage Timmy to play with an educational toy rather than watch television. If he finds it reinforcing, he will frequently play quietly with his toys. This incident is an example of verbal praise, which is considered a *social reinforcer*.

I believe that verbal praise is one of the most important types of reinforcers. Associated with hugs, kisses, and other forms of loving physical contact, it is the essence of catching kids being good. You must begin as early as possible to indicate high regard and faith in your children by always affirming their positive traits. That doesn't mean that you should use phony praise when it is not appropriate. You can praise your children if you have realistic expectations and engage them in activities that are commensurate with their individual abilities.

Don't praise children for trying things they can't do. For instance, when three-year-old Sara tries to adjust the water temperature while taking a bath, even though the act reflects independence and initiative (both desirable traits), you wouldn't praise her. She could easily get scalded, so you would tell her that hot water could hurt her. Because she is not yet developmentally ready or physically capable of the subtle controls needed to adjust the flow of water, you could simply divert her by bringing her attention to a bath toy. Or you could tell her that it's your job to take care of the water now but that Sara can adjust the water when she is bigger.

Social reinforcers include positive statements, words and looks of approval, smiles, and laughter. They should also include hugs, kisses, and pats on the back, all of which communicate approval and high regard for the child.

When children are engaged in new or difficult academic activities or are playing sports, high regard is demonstrated by positive comments such as "You can handle it" and "I know you can do it." If the child fails, you can say things such as "That's OK, we will work on it" and "You will get it, just keep trying." But the most important message is "Don't worry, because I love you whether you do it or not. Just keep trying because you want to, not because you think I will not love you if you don't do it."

In addition to verbal or other social reinforcers, you can also use other types of *external reinforcers*. For example, if seven-year-old Jason is having trouble with his spelling homework and has started to avoid doing it, you might say to him, "Tell you what, Jason. Every Thursday night, before your weekly spelling test on Friday, I will give you 25 cents for each word you can spell correctly. That way, if you get all ten words correct you will have an extra $2.50 for the weekend." Or if seventeen-year-old Craig has not been doing his major chore of taking out the trash, you might say to him, "Craig, each week, if you take out the trash both days without me having to ask you to do it, I will let you have the car for an extra three hours on the weekend." Having more access to the family car is a particularly powerful external reinforcer for most adolescents.

In the case of Craig, use of the car may be a more powerful reinforcer than money, praise from his parents, or anything else his parents could think of. This is a very important point. If a reward does not work, it is not reinforcing. Go back to the drawing board and find out from the kid what would be reinforcing and also reasonable.

Negative Reinforcement

How can removing something work to reward behavior? The concept of negative reinforcement, shown in the lower left-hand quadrant of the table, is often confusing even to experienced psychologists.

Without going into the linguistic and scientific reasons for this confusion (which is partly due to the way the words *negative* and *reinforcement* seem to contradict each other), let me see if I can explain it. Negative reinforcement works on the principle that good behaviors can be increased by allowing a child to escape or avoid an unpleasant or aversive situation. When you remove unpleasantness, you can increase good behavior. For example, if Johnny dislikes his daily chore of washing dishes and you say, "Johnny, you do not have to wash the dishes tonight if you will write the report that is due next week," you will probably increase the chance that he will write the report.

Negative reinforcement also explains how a lot of misbehavior is maintained or reinforced. The best example is the parent who frequently gives in to a child's demands or noncompliant behavior. Here is how this works. You tell five-year-old Susan to brush her teeth before going to bed every night. Susan's refusals are accompanied by whining, crying, and tantrums. You can't stand her whining (it is aversive to you). Sometimes when it is late, there's a lot of work to do, and Susan needs to get to bed, you give in and allow her to go to bed without brushing her teeth.

In other words, you are negatively reinforced (dropping the demand that Susan brush her teeth stops the whining that you can't stand). But Susan has been positively reinforced for whining and crying, because by doing that she doesn't have to brush her teeth. When this type of child-parent interaction persists, children quickly learn how to avoid fulfilling even simple parental requests.

Response Cost

Response cost might be considered a sort of hybrid of positive re-inforcement and punishment. For example, your child might start the week off with a set amount of "tokens" (these may be in the form of stars, stickers, or anything else that might work for you). The tokens may represent money (maybe a nickel) or a unit that is used toward earning special time or trips with one or both parents. For each misbehavior, your child loses one token. At the end of the week your child cashes in the tokens for money or whatever else is being used as a reinforcer. In other words, you give the child a reward at the beginning of the week with the expectation that the child will be able to keep the reward. This might be perceived as a punishment in the sense that the child is losing something of value for each misbehavior, but it is also a form of positive reinforcement because the child is receiving something of value as encourage-ment. I find that this technique can be successful with children who frequently misbehave, but it works best when it is used both at home and school.

In using reinforcers, you must sit down with the child and make up the menu of things the child wants, that is, things that are re-wards to the child, not what you think should be rewarding. Also, you may want to set the program up with your child's teacher, so that both home and school are providing reinforcers for school-related misbehaviors such as failure to do schoolwork or homework. Addi-tionally, I often use a variation of positive reinforcers and response cost with actual money. Bonus tokens and money can be earned for outstanding acts, such as when a child offers to help or does some-thing nice for a peer, sibling, or parent. At the end of the week, tokens or checks on a paper are exchanged at home for money or are added to the pool of money saved to purchase something.

The reward system must be in writing and fully understood by adults and children. Students at home and school can earn or lose a predetermined number of tokens for each behavior. The system fails if the child can manipulate it or if the adult is arbitrary or inconsistent in following the rules. Here is an example of a problem and how to set up a reinforcement system.

How to Set Up a Reward System

Seven-year-old Scott was driving his teachers and parents crazy. His teacher was sure that he had Attention-Deficit Hyperactivity Disorder (ADHD) because he couldn't seem to sit still in class. He was oppositional, frequently fidgeted, got out of his seat often to wander around the room and always seemed to have his hands on other kids. Mrs. Johnson, his mother, claimed that every request she made of Scott ended up in a power struggle. For instance, Scott resisted getting up in time for school, playing cooperatively and sharing with his five-year-old sister, turning off the television when requested, and going to bed on time.

When Mr. and Mrs. Johnson described their problems to me, it was obvious that they had different opinions. Mr. Johnson was generally successful in obtaining immediate compliance because he either threatened or gave Scott a "good spanking." But as Mrs. Johnson pointed out, the misbehavior continued. Mr. Johnson claimed that since his wife stopped spanking, Scott had gotten worse.

Mrs. Johnson admitted that she gave up quite frequently because she couldn't stand the conflict. Often she yelled, pleaded, and threatened. However, she realized that screaming and yelling were just as ineffective as spanking.

Family history and a detailed developmental and social history of Scott suggested the possibility of ADHD, but I felt that the inconsistency in parenting should be corrected before we attempted an extensive trial of various doses of Ritalin. Even if he did have ADHD, he would still require behavioral intervention. I explained how the cycle of misbehavior, spanking, giving in, screaming, yelling, and oppositional responses from Scott were reinforcing his oppositional behavior. I also explained that spanking was not a punishment because it did not cause Scott to discontinue the behaviors. Scott's main reinforcement in this cycle was that he was in control.

Once Scott's parents understood the ineffectiveness of their punishment procedures, we agreed to implement a behavioral system that would include both the home and the school. To begin, the Johnsons agreed that they would ignore minor misbehaviors so that Scott would not be reinforced for the attention he got from them. They would discontinue spanking, screaming, yelling, and negative statements that either directly or indirectly told Scott he was a bad kid. They would use withdrawal of privileges and time-outs as the major punishments.

The focus of their efforts would be to reinforce good behavior by catching Scott being good and praising him, and by implementing an extrinsic reward system. Once Scott agreed to a written contract, they made up a reinforcement menu based on his requests. Each week Scott would earn points. At the end of the week, the points could be cashed in for the rewards that he chose. If Scott did not misbehave once on any one day, he could earn 20 points. Theoretically, he could earn 140 points (7×20) if he didn't misbehave all week.

Examples of rewards on the menu included an adventure for three hours with his father on Sunday afternoon (100 points), a trip to the local ice cream store just with his mother (80 points), a new Nintendo game (300 points), a Power Ranger figure (50 points), staying up an extra hour on Saturday night (30 points), and five dollars to spend at a toy store any way he wants (200 points).

This case is meant to provide an example. You need to adjust the number of points and the rewards according to the child's age and desires. For instance, a plan like this one only works when the child is mature enough to understand and plan ahead to save points over several weeks to get a high-cost item. Because of limited attention and memory, younger children may need a plan that features low points for small rewards that they receive each day. Older children and adolescents may be better reinforced with actual money rather than points. Or points and money can be interchangeable—

a ten-year-old may be willing to save up a lot of points to buy a new skateboard, while a teenager may be really motivated to earn points over a year for a car.

We decided to use both positive reinforcement and response cost to implement the program for Scott. Exhibit 6.1 shows the contract Scott's parents worked out with their son and his teacher.

Exhibit 6.1 is only meant to provide an example of how to write a contract. Each behavior should be described in terms that everybody understands. Some type of chart should be constructed so that everyone can see the daily progress. There will be times that children will claim that parents are being unfair or when they deny that they misbehaved. These incidents will have to be negotiated calmly and rationally, and if necessary, the contract may have to be tuned up from time to time. Also, reinforcers may have to be changed if they are no longer rewarding to the child.

Punishing

Now that we have talked about a reward system, let's consider the effective use of punishment, if it becomes necessary. Like reward systems, there are two kinds of punishment systems: one in which you give something and one in which you remove something. The types of punishments that fall into the first category are things such as verbal reprimands, imposing unpleasant consequences, or withdrawing privileges. Withdrawing privileges is a punishment because the intent is to take something away that the child plans to have. This is a little different from a deprivation punishment such as time-out, in which you immediately remove the child from a pleasant situation.

Punishment as defined here is something you do to a child that decreases the misbehavior preceding it. Parental punishments include any actions that children find unpleasant. Verbal reprimands are punishments if they stop a misbehavior. I have found that reprimands only work when they are used sparingly and do not

EXHIBIT 6.1 Sample Reward System Contract.

Johnson Contract

We the undersigned agree to the following conditions to help Scott improve his behavior in home and school. Mom and Dad agree that they will try to stop spanking and screaming. Scott agrees that he will try his best to earn points for the things that he wants, which are outlined in this contract. Mrs. Smith [Scott's teacher] agrees that she will tally points each day and send them home at the end of the week.

Response Cost: Mom and Dad agree to place 140 points in "the bank" every Sunday night. Scott agrees that he will lose points each time he does the following:

- One refusal to do what Mom, Dad, or Mrs. Smith ask—lose 5 points. This includes adult requests to go to bed on time, return to his seat in school, take his hands off other kids, get up when his mother tells him it's time, play cooperatively and share with his sister, and turn off the television.
- Second refusal—lose 12 points
- Third refusal—lose 15 points
- More refusals—lose 20 points (the whole day's supply)

Positive Reinforcement: Scott will receive 10 points for each of the following:

- One half hour of working quietly at his desk in school
- Getting up without his mother's request
- Going to bed on time without Mom or Dad asking
- Initiating cooperative play with his sister
- Doing something nice with his sister (such as watching her favorite TV show with her)
- Offering to help Mom or Dad with a chore

include demeaning statements. Although screaming and yelling can be punishing when used occasionally, they rapidly lose effect the more they are used. For instance, if screaming at your three-year-old once or twice for running out into the road stops that behavior, you can assume that screaming was punishing. However, if your child continues to run into the road and you continue to scream, forget it. Stop screaming, and use praise and reward to teach the child not to run into the street.

As I mentioned earlier, school suspension is a great example of a punishment that is often a nonpunishment. If a child receives frequent in- or out-of-school suspensions for particular misbehaviors and those misbehaviors do not decrease, it is obvious that suspension is not a punishment. Many students I have worked with love to be suspended, even if their parents impose additional punishments, because it gets them out of classes or schools they hate. The most patently absurd use of suspension is as a punishment for truancy or class cutting!

On the plus side, punishment may be effective when a variety of positive techniques don't work. Punishment can produce very quick short-term results. Some psychologists make a case for the use of carefully controlled aversive procedures to reduce extremely self-injurious and aggressive behaviors—they recommend procedures such as the use of mild electric shock, slapping, water sprayed in the face, or other noxious stimuli. However, the research tends to show that even with the most dangerous behavior, this kind of punishment doesn't generalize to other situations or places and invariably it is overused. So what types of punishments should you use? Here are some examples.

Deprivation Punishment or Time-Out

It is very important to understand deprivation punishment because it is the basis for time-out. Time-out works by removing the child from a positive situation, thereby increasing the probability that the child will want to act appropriately when returned to the positive situation.

A 1992 poll showed that 38 percent of parents responded that they used time-out and preferred it to spanking. This is an 18 percent increase over a similar poll in 1962 and reflects a positive trend in parental discipline in America. But time-out—a negative punishment—is too widely misunderstood and too often abused.

When properly used, time-out serves to remove children from a pleasant activity such as play, family functions, or television. As with other types of punishment, this approach should result in a decrease in the misbehavior for which it is used. It is only appropriate for children under the ages of six or seven and will only work if the child is removed to a dull or unpleasant setting.

The rule of thumb is that the removal time in minutes should not exceed the child's age. However, the research on effectiveness shows that the correct duration is best determined by what works. Short periods of time-out can be very effective when used in conjunction with positive reinforcement programs.

There are several types of time-out. When you put your child in a chair away from the rest of the family and facing a wall, it is called *exclusionary* time-out. *Nonexclusionary* time-out is accomplished by sitting your child away from the family but in a position to watch without participating. *Isolation* occurs when your child is temporarily removed from social interaction to another room or place. Any of these can be effective depending on the child and the circumstances.

Here is an example of the correct use of time-out. Four-year-old Billy is playing with his three-year-old sister (a positive experience for him) but won't share one of the toys with her. He hits her when she tries to get it. You calmly and quietly say, "Billy, you know what happens when you hit your sister. You must go to time-out." You remove him from the play situation (pleasant experience for him) and put him in a chair facing the wall in the kitchen for three minutes (he is deprived of playing with his sister for what seems to you like a very short time, but feels like half an hour to a four-year-old). When the punishment is over, you say, "You have been a good boy for staying in time-out. Now you can play with your sister, and I know you will share." He will return to the pleasant situation, knowing that he will again be removed if he hits his sister.

As an expert witness, I have dealt with too many abuses of time-out in schools. Long periods of time-out (over thirty minutes) are unethical and should not be allowed. Further, you should be very concerned if your child's teacher uses an enclosure such as a cardboard box, a wooden booth, cloakroom, closet, or any other situation that is not well ventilated and lighted and where the child cannot be directly observed. The presence of such enclosures all too often leads to improper use and overuse. They may be necessary for very aggressive and self-injurious children, but this usually occurs in special school settings and should be carefully supervised to maintain the child's health and safety.

Time-out should replace spanking as your last-resort, heavy-duty punishment for toddlers and young children. It should be reserved for extreme behaviors such as hitting, cursing, or lying. Other daily irritants should not be punished with time-out. As with yelling or raising your voice, if time-out becomes routine, it will lose its effectiveness.

Time-out is only effective if the child is removed from a desired place or activity to an undesired place. If you send five-year-old Sally to her room (where she has a television set and most of her toys), it may not work. Also, the process of putting your child in time-out should not be reinforcing. For instance, if four-year-old Ken is in a power struggle with you and you respond by yelling, screaming, and putting him in a time-out where he won't stay, you have been defeated.

Here is a list of dos and don'ts for the effective use of time-out:

- Do establish clear procedures and time limits for going to and remaining in time-out.

- Do tell your child what rules have been broken, and calmly request that he or she go to time-out.
- When explaining time-out, use a timer to show the child how long it is. Use the timer during time-out.
- Do prepare options if your child refuses time-out.

Calmly repeat those options, and if your child refuses, take time to consider what to do. One option could be a more severe punishment such as no television for the rest of the day or for the child's favorite show.

- If your child refuses to go to time-out, calmly hold him or her in a basket hold in the time-out place, and quietly remind the child why he or she is there and that you will let go if he or she agrees to stay in time-out. (Chapter Seven describes and illustrates how to do a basket hold.)
- Don't yell, scream, or threaten your children when you send them to time-out.
- If you send your child to his or her room, don't forget that the child is there.

In conclusion, time-out should be used as part of a total reinforcement system. If you are using it three or four times a week for the same misbehaviors, it is not working because it is no longer a punishment. Stop, and try to figure out the cause of the misbehavior. At this point, the child's misbehavior may be a way of getting your attention, so you are actually rewarding the child by using time-out. Also, make sure you save it for only the most undesirable behaviors. If it still doesn't work, your best bet is to strengthen the reward system to motivate the child to behave.

Overcorrection

Overcorrection is a type of punishment that can be very effective in the short term while it also establishes long-term positive patterns. It uses two stages. In the first stage, restitution is accomplished by correcting negative effects of the misbehavior. Then during positive practice, the child practices more appropriate behaviors, usually in an exaggerated fashion. For instance, for two weeks, thirteen-year-old Mike has been calling his eleven-year-old brother Bill a sleazeball. He is required to apologize verbally and in writing, and for three weeks, whenever he speaks or refers to his brother, he must use Bill's name. If he refuses, he is grounded until he complies.

Withdrawal of Privileges

A popular and frequently effective punishment with older children is withdrawal of privileges. Grounding is one example. For instance, seventeen-year-old Jimmy comes home two hours past curfew on Saturday night. He loses the privilege of going out next Saturday night and the use of the family car for a week.

But what if his parents really lose it when he gets home late and decide on a draconian punishment. They scream, "Since you came in late last night you can't go out for the next six months!" Is this going to work? Are they really going to be able to enforce their edict? As with time-out, if Jimmy's parents overuse the punishment, are unable to really enforce it, or are repeatedly grounding him even for short periods, it is obviously not a punishment because it hasn't stopped his misbehavior. At that point it has become a power struggle—and Jimmy is winning.

The most popular but least effective attempts at punishment include yelling, screaming, nagging, blaming, criticizing, and various types of putdowns. Even though we all know these usually don't work, we all use them. They are probably the most frequent parental and teacher responses to misbehavior. I have school data showing that these too often become emotionally abusive. Frequent use of these techniques to punish children can cause lifelong emotional problems.

Now that we have discussed the major aspects of extrinsic rewards and punishments, let us consider another approach to motivating children.

How to Be a Democratic Parent Without Being a Wimp

Let's get something straight before we begin this discussion of democracy in the home. Do not confuse democratic parents either with wimps or with permissive and misguided caretakers who want to be buddies with their children and are afraid to set limits. If you scored below the average on the Parent Punitiveness Quiz, you probably lean toward democratic parenting. But what is democratic parenting and why has it had such a bad rap for so long? Let me start with a little history.

Before and during World War II, the rise of fascism was one of the factors that caused many Americans to question and challenge authoritarian practices throughout our culture. Many realized that while we espoused the democratic ideals embodied in our Constitution and Bill of Rights, we made few attempts to model or teach the actual processes of crucial values such as individual rights, the uniqueness of individuals, justice, due process, and cooperation.

Yes, in schools we were taught about democracy through coursework. But while democracy was being taught from textbooks, most administrators and teachers were running schools as autocracies, never involving students meaningfully in the processes of democracy. Students rarely experienced or practiced important features of democracy such as due process or the opportunity for legitimate means of dissent. Homes were typically run by fathers who frequently used authoritarian methods of child rearing, including physical force—a hallmark of totalitarian regimes.

In reaction to these discrepancies between theory and practice, democratic methods of schooling and child rearing were promoted by prominent philosophers such as John Dewey, physicians such as Dr. Spock, and psychologists such as Carl Rogers. They all emphasized that children's learning should be experiential. Education and life are inseparable, and therefore schools and parents should teach practical skills, inquiry, and the process of democracy. Self-discipline, freedom, and the relativity of values, truth, and morality should be stressed over dogma and fundamentalism. Children in a democracy should learn to think and act on their own.

The principles of democratic child rearing were intertwined with the humanistic thinking that pervades the Constitution and Bill of Rights. Humanism espouses the concept that children are born with an innate capacity or ability to do good and to become competent. Parents and teachers should encourage and guide children, rather than teach or force ideas into them. These concepts led to what some considered excessively permissive parenting, a concept with which Americans periodically flirt. However, the fusion and confusion of democratic parenting, humanism, and permissiveness has led to the idea that democratic parents should not set limits, discipline their kids, or teach values.

But societies all set limits. It is how the limits are set that distinguishes a democracy. Laws are made by elected officials with participation by citizens at all levels. If citizens don't like the rules, they can throw out the scoundrels who make them. Now, of course, as a parent you weren't elected. But that doesn't mean that you can't encourage your children at all age levels to participate in setting rules. The purpose of this approach is to elicit a sense of family community and ownership of the rules and a sense of the power of cooperation and prosocial behavior over competition and manipulation of others. It stresses empathy, caring, and discipline based on the value of being good for the sake of goodness rather than on fear of punishment.

Even though the emphasis is on trust and responsibility, there may be times when you, as the parent, must take over. When limits are tested, you can still respect your child's rights, but not at the expense of the rights of others. But you do this through reasoning and appeal to how one child's behavior affects everyone. If the misbehavior doesn't stop after all preventive and positive corrective measures are taken, then (as in the real world) punishment may be used.

Common Misbehaviors and How to Handle Them

Democratic parenting begins as early as the child is able to understand words. From the very beginning, rules should be explained through reasoning, persuasion, and distraction. Here are some examples of the wrong and correct ways to deal with common misbehaviors at different age levels. Each is a composite of many cases I have seen over the years.

Eighteen-month-old Julia reaches for her father's razor, which has fallen from the sink.
- Authoritarian Dad smacks Julia on the wrist and yells, "Don't ever touch that razor again!"
- Democratic Dad presents Julia with one of her bath toys as he grabs the razor and says, "Julia, that's a no no—it can give you a boo boo [her word for pain]."

In the correct version, Dad has laid the groundwork for Julia to expect to hear reasons why not to behave in a certain way while at the same time being given a positive option.

Eight-year-old Randy and Judy, his seven-year-old sister, are fighting over who should use the swing.
- Authoritarian Mom, disgusted with the bickering, says, "Either you two take turns or you will go into the house and no one will use the swing!"
- Democratic Mom says, "OK, kids, let's see if we can work this out. Tell me what happened."

Judy cries, "I was here first. Randy tried to kick me off the swing." Randy replies, "Yeah, but she got to use the swing all week and I haven't had a chance. It isn't fair."

Mom turns to Judy, "Is that true, Judy?" Judy denies this and continues to cry. Mom says, "Well, I am not going to take sides about who is right or wrong because I know that in your own way each of you thinks the other is unfair. But we are going to sit down and decide how you two can share the swing. We will make up some rules, which I will write down. Then if you disagree we will use the rules to settle the matter."

Fourteen-year-old Jarad claims that all of his friends are allowed to stay out until midnight. His parents do not feel this is appropriate for a fourteen-year-old.

• Authoritarian Dad says, "I don't care what your friends' parents do. They are not your parents and we will tell you what to do. You will be home by ten o'clock or you will be grounded for a month each time you break the rule."

• Democratic Dad says, "I know that you want to be like the other kids, but we really worry when you are out that late. Do you know why we worry?"

Jarad responds, "You just think I'm still a baby. Nothing is going to happen to me. I'm not a little kid anymore."

"You haven't answered the question. Why do we worry when you are out that late?"

"None of the other kids' parents worry. I guess you think I'm doing something wrong. Like, maybe you think I am snorting coke or dropping acid. I don't know, maybe you are worried that something will happen to me. But don't worry; I can take care of myself."

Democratic Mom: "Well we do worry. I think we need to negotiate this issue. We need to have a family council to discuss this when we are all calm and rational. But before we do, I would like to call or meet with your friends' parents to see if they really don't care if their kids are out until midnight."

"Come on Mom, that would be totally embarrassing. All the kids would be really mad at you and probably at me."

"Well, I don't want to embarrass you, but either we negotiate this in a reasonable way or we can just decide for you. You know that we always try to reason things out, but if you don't want to negotiate, it is up to you."

At this point, parents and Jarad will negotiate the contact with the other kids and their parents. Mom and Dad believe that the other parents are not happy about such a late curfew but don't know how to handle the problem. But before his parents call the others about a meeting, they agree that Jarad will have the chance to warn his buddies and tell them that he has no choice in the matter so he can save face.

Before the meeting, Jarad and his parents have a family council and negotiate a preliminary agreement. Jarad can stay out until 11 P.M. as long as he is at a friend's house where parents are home. If he plans to leave where he is, he must call and get approval. If his parents don't approve because they are afraid for his safety, they will come and get him. If they do approve, he is to call them when he arrives. A condition he doesn't like, but agrees to, is that his parents must have the address and telephone number where he will be and the name of anyone who drives him anywhere. They all agree that if Jarad is responsible and there are few infractions, they will renegotiate when he is fifteen.

When the parents meet, Jarad's friends are given the option of being there. They opt to attend, even though they all complain to their parents and are angry at Jarad's parents. However, all the parents are happy to commiserate with each other. Based on the democratic model provided, they agree to a mutual plan. On the one hand the kids are not happy, but they grudgingly agree that parents have the right to worry about their children's safety and also have a right to know where they are. On the other hand the parents have recognized that their kids are growing up and have a right to some autonomy.

How to Run a Family Council

The core of democratic child rearing is the family council. This is a periodic meeting when all family members congregate to discuss how they feel, what they want, and how to resolve problems. Councils can be informal and do not have to be run according to Robert's

Rules. Over the years I have developed a specific format that borrows from theory and pragmatic aspects of participatory democracy, family therapy techniques, and mental health principles.

You can institute family councils as soon as children are able to sit and begin to learn to reason and problem solve. However, it is crucial that the length, timing, and level of decision making be commensurate with the children's developmental level. For instance, you couldn't expect most five-year-olds to sit for an hour and discuss what time they must go to bed. Besides the limited attention span of most five-year-olds, you know how many hours of sleep the child needs, and that is really not negotiable. However, even though the child really doesn't yet understand the concept of the passage of time, you might negotiate in terms of which television shows the child can watch before going to bed, how quick and cooperative the child is about bath time, the time you will spend reading to the child in bed, weekdays versus weekends, and corresponding bedtimes based on age so that older children stay up later. With developmental factors in mind, here are some guidelines for running family councils.

- *At the first meeting, prepare a set of written guidelines about how the meeting should run.* These are not written in stone and can be modified when necessary. But they can't be changed between meetings or arbitrarily by one person, because they represent consensus.
- *Set a regular time to meet.* This can be weekly, monthly, or whatever is necessary, but the meeting should be planned ahead, unless an emergency arises. Many families set aside time on Saturday or Sunday morning, when the stresses of work and school are less acute than during the week.
- *Only one person can speak at a time.* Everyone gets an equal turn to speak.
- *Participants must be free to express honestly how they feel.* This means if a child is angry at a parent, the child should be allowed to express that anger. Each family will have to decide appropriate levels of language. As a therapist and parent, I have no problem with

obscenities if they are the best and most genuine way the person is able to express feeling. Of course, this is only allowed during the session.

You may not be comfortable with my guidelines for the use of obscene language. You have the right to forbid specific words or expressions that defile your family values. If you decide to permit complete freedom of expression, the child must understand that you are allowing obscene language during family council because it serves a purpose. If cursing is just used gratuitously to test the limits, or outside the council, consequences should be discussed.

• *What is said in council stays there and can only be brought up again either at the next meeting or if all parties agree to discuss it outside of council.* This precludes parents or children from plotting ways to manipulate future meetings.

• *All plans or agreements should be in writing.* There should be agreed-upon sanctions or consequences for those who break the agreements.

• *Parents should model problem solving at the meetings.* The basic steps include (1) identifying, defining, and naming the problem, (2) gathering all the necessary information about the problem, (3) brainstorming potential solutions, (4) implementing a solution, (5) discussing how well the solution works, (6) praising and encouraging the parties who implement the solution, and (7) choosing another solution if your original one doesn't work or ceases to be effective. There are many cognitive-behavioral and Adlerian programs that teach problem solving, and it is a good idea to explore such programs if your family meetings don't seem effective.

During meetings all family members should practice listening and feedback skills like those discussed in Chapter Five. Participants can also practice complimenting, praising, and reinforcing each other. They can learn about how each perceives and interprets the world, and they can even do role-playing where they literally change sides. For instance, if Dad can't stand nine-year-old Nina's constant whining when she does not get what she wants, they can reverse roles. Dad, playing Nina, asks Nina for $100. Nina says she does not have it. It could go like this:

DAD PLAYING NINA: Come on Dad, give me a hundred dollars.

NINA PLAYING DAD: I don't have it.

DAD PLAYING NINA: Oh, I know you must have it.

NINA PLAYING DAD: (*Getting impatient.*) I said I don't have it.

DAD PLAYING NINA: (*Whining and pulling on Nina's sleeve.*) That's not faiiir. You're meeeann. Oh, come on, Dad. You promised.

NINA PLAYING DAD: (*Starting to get angry.*) I never promised. Leave me alone. Stop grabbing me. (*In her own voice.*) I don't act that way!

Often, in this sort of role-playing, someone starts to laugh. The parents hope that after she cools down, Nina will realize what it is like for her dad to be nagged by her.

• *In determining solutions and rules for the family to live by, emphasize justness and fairness.* This is more effective than a punitive "law and order" approach. Rules should allow for individual and developmental differences and provide for extenuating circumstances in the use of punishment.

• *If you write contracts, clearly spell out behaviors and consequences.* You can use the behavioral techniques I discussed earlier.

• *Focus on major issues and moral decisions facing your children.* Rather than making absolute pronouncements about right and wrong, good and evil, help children to understand the meaning and consequences of what you consider to be immoral behavior. You can use parables, metaphors, and little stories about real life or even fairy tales and fables to illustrate and teach.

It sounds like a lot of work, doesn't it? Teaching problem-solving skills, rational thinking, and moral reasoning takes time and patience. If necessary, you may have to replace your own authoritarian, directive, and controlling behaviors. You may have to model respect and understanding for everyone's views and feelings even if you don't agree with them. You must teach and show cooperation, discussion, and compromise. You may have to give fewer lectures and ask more questions. You will learn to give choices instead of edicts.

The techniques I suggest for family councils motivate children to follow the rules, make high-quality decisions, develop closer, warmer relationships with you, and build good self-esteem, self-confidence, self-discipline, and a sense of control over their lives. That's not a bad payoff for some intensive effort as your children are growing up, is it?

7

Anger and Resentment

In the discussion on transgenerational patterns of child rearing, I showed you how expressions of emotion can be passed on through the process of modeling. If you deal with frustration by screaming, losing your temper, and hitting, there is a good chance that one, some, or all of your children will learn the same behavior.

Because misbehavior and parental discipline so often involve expressions of strong emotions, it is important for you to understand how this occurs and how to control undesirable feelings when disciplining your children. This is especially true because evidence indicates that spanking is almost always accompanied by negative feelings by spanker and spankee.

The behavioral explanation of the role of modeling in determining how the expression of emotions is taught tells only part of the story. From an ecological-systems perspective, many factors affect how parents deal with the stress that can be associated with children's misbehavior. For instance, biology can mediate the way you and your children deal with misbehavior. Some types of depression, anxiety, and psychosis seem to have a genetic basis and can't be ignored as they influence discipline. Also, the physical manifestations of certain hereditary traits can cause parents or children to develop predisposers of misbehavior such as low self-esteem, poor impulse control, social isolation, or antisocial anger at authorities and peers.

Some children are born with physical deformities, unattractive facial features, or even the predisposition to obesity. They may be ridiculed, scorned, or unconsciously rejected by parents, siblings, and others. For instance, some children with a hereditary predisposition to obesity may be blamed for their body weight. This, in combination with other factors, may result in misbehavior, frustration, and a lifetime of discrimination.

Traits such as obesity in both sexes and shortness in boys affect adulthood. People in either category are less likely to marry, more likely to live in poverty, and more likely to earn far less than those who do not have these traits. Also, studies show that teachers tend to be more positive to students who are physically attractive than those who are not. So, as a parent, you need to be aware of how biological and physical factors may affect your emotions and feelings when you discipline your children. Here are a few factors to consider.

The Role of Temperament

There is good evidence that everyone is born with a genetically determined temperament. Both your own and your childrens' temperaments determine how you all deal with misbehavior and accompanying emotions such as anger, anxiety, and disgust. But these traits do not operate in a vacuum nor do they have absolute control over how you act. You can control how you express inherited traits. This is especially important if your traits don't match or fit well with those of your child.

It is always desirable to try to modify the effects of your temperament so that your actions fit well with your childrens' abilities, motivations, and opportunities. Examples of inherited traits that play an important role in discipline are *adaptability*, the ability to change behavior when needed; *mood*, the level and intensity of feelings; *activity*, the amount of physical motion during sleeping, eating, and playing; and *distractibility*, the ability or lack of ability to remain focused on an activity.

Problems occur when parents and children have a bad match between temperaments. For instance, if you generally have a low activity level and your child is always on the move, it may be very difficult for you to keep up. Or if you have a low level of persistence and are generally highly distractible, you will find it even more difficult than usual to cope with a child with Attention-Deficit Hyperactivity Disorder. In both these cases it is unlikely that you will always be consistent, patient, and persistent in setting and maintaining limits.

Caregivers may tend be less warm and helpful to children who are temperamentally less persistent, more active, and more distractible than others. For instance, research shows that teachers are more critical of children who display low attention and high distractibility.

The point here is that if you need to learn to express your emotions more appropriately in disciplining your child, be sure to begin with an examination of your basic temperament and that of your child. Review the traits discussed here and determine if any describe you. You may have a poor fit with your child if you find that you are frequently impatient and angry at your child's misbehaviors, even minor indiscretions. Inappropriate parental expression of anger is the most destructive force in maintaining positive discipline. Of course, other behaviors such as neglect, rejection, and withholding of love are also bad, but they all reflect some level of anger. So let's talk about anger.

Dealing with Anger: Yours and Your Child's

Anger, a feeling that extends from irritability to rage, can be one of the most dangerous and destructive emotions you feel when reacting to your child's misbehavior. Anger may lead to responses ranging from sarcasm, name calling, and putdowns to screaming, spanking, and crippling physical assault. But before what I said sends you into a spasm of guilt, you must realize that almost all parents, except perhaps those slated for sainthood, have experienced anger about their children's defiance, oppositional behavior, and misdeeds.

Anger is not inherently bad. It is an emotion that can arise as a result of any conflict in life, even those between you and your child. Conflict is a normal part of life and a potentially positive force to promote personal growth and social change. In any healthy relationship there will be times when your requests and your child's responses clash. It is therefore crucial that you and your child learn ways to handle your anger when conflicts occur.

Some types of anger are justified. For instance, anger at five-year-old Annie for bullying her three-year-old brother is not bad. However, how you react is what may cause the problem.

Anger often accompanies hostility, aggression, and assertion. *Hostility* is a general level of negative feeling about a person, idea, or entity. It is an attitude that can lead to angry verbal expressions or aggressive outbursts. If you are generally hostile to your child, you may always respond to any level of misbehavior by yelling or hitting.

Aggression, by definition, is an overt physical or verbal attack. Aggression implies an intent to hurt. Despite disclaimers by many, spanking is inherently an aggressive attack. Ask children who have been spanked if it hurt. Initially, they may deny it, state that they deserved it, or claim that their parents only wanted to teach them a lesson. But if you question them further, they will admit that the spanking hurt and made them angry.

Assertiveness is an action meant to protect your own integrity and self-worth and standing up for what you know is right as a parent. Assertion implies that you are in control but are not using your position to hurt or injure anyone. As opposed to aggressive parents, assertive parents allow children to question the rationale for discipline.

Unfortunately, assertion and aggression may be interpreted as being the same. But there is a reason for this. For at least four decades, starting around the 1930s, parents were blamed for every childhood deviance from bed wetting to schizophrenia. Blame was deduced from psychoanalytic interpretation of parenting. Perhaps in reaction to parental stigmatization, in the 1970s, a group of behaviorally oriented psychologists told parents to forget guilt and become more assertive. Parents were exhorted to take control of their children and show them who is boss. As a result, assertiveness training entered the realm of pop psychology.

The assertiveness movement helped train many parents to clarify the differences between assertion and aggression. But unfortunately, I have seen many parents who are so anxious to shed the mantle of self-blame for their children's misbehavior that they blame their children for everything. They justify aggression as if it were assertion. But anger is never an adequate justification for aggressive parenting. Therefore every parent should begin with an understanding of their own sources of anger.

Is Anger an Inborn Part of Your Nature?

I can't count the times that a parent or child has told me, "But, Dr. Hyman, that is the way I am. I guess I was born that way. I have always had a temper and I don't think there is much I can do about it." Wrong! I don't think inappropriate expressions of anger are inborn, except in rare cases of brain dysfunction caused by heredity or prenatal damage. In fact, while we all have the potential to get angry, the expression of anger is often defined by our culture. For instance, the Hopi Indian culture stresses cooperation and peaceful coexistence and has peaceful gods. In contrast, the Maoris of New Zealand have warlike gods and various expressions of anger are considered a way of proving manhood. The Inuits of Alaska and northern Canada didn't have a word for aggression, and expressions of anger were considered abnormal and dealt with by laughter rather than counter anger.

In the United States, anger is generally disapproved in the workplace and in school. But it is valued and highly ritualized for spectators and athletes in sports such as football, hockey, and boxing. Unfortunately, the generally controlled anger of trained athletes is not mirrored by fans, who sometimes riot over what happens on the playing field. Research shows that the relative incidence of homicides increases in the metropolitan areas of losing teams after NFL playoff games. Frustration apparently leads to anger that results in aggression.

A Brief History of Anger

Did you know that during the Victorian era, children were perceived as innocent, and anger was an unacceptable emotion? The slightest show of anger required firm discipline. From the late nineteenth century through the years between World War I and World War II, psychologists began to recognize that children could and did become angry. Rather than suppress the emotion, teachers and parents were encouraged to teach children to channel their anger into more acceptable behaviors, such as competition or moral indignation. But teachers were much less supportive of this approach than parents. Anger in the classroom interrupted a busy schedule of teaching.

Mothers have never been big supporters of channeling anger because aggression by females has generally been disapproved in our society. But fathers have generally liked to see channeled anger. Fathers expected children to be aggressive and spunky. Paradoxically, parents severely punished their children for expressing anger toward them but were relatively tolerant of anger when it was directed against peers.

Following World War II, the psychoanalytic school still felt that it was appropriate to teach children to channel their angry feelings. Psychotherapy for angry children provided experiences for them to *abreact* or "work out" their anger. They were encouraged to punch plastic blow-up dolls, to hit, bang, and twist dolls that represented parents or siblings with whom they were angry, and to use creative arts such as puppet play to get out their anger.

During the 1940s and 1950s, psychologists began to posit that anger was learned and often resulted from frustration. Frustration led to the ultimate expression of anger, which was aggression.

Behaviorists examined the role of imitation and learning in the development of anger. Research showed that children who were exposed to angry models were more likely to express anger themselves. Because anger is learned, it can be unlearned. Treatment programs involved reinforcing children's nonangry responses and ignoring angry responses. Behaviorists felt that encouraging children to be aggressive in therapy did not solve any problems.

As I have said many times in this book, I believe that children do learn, generally from parents, how to express their anger. They develop internal dialogues that tell them to respond with anger to certain types of incidents. These dialogues stay with them—and are the prompters of angry responses when the children become parents themselves. The purpose here is to help you deal with your own angry feelings that flavor the way you discipline your child.

Controlling and Appropriately Expressing Your Anger

Mrs. Rand had a problem. Her husband, Mr. Rand, was increasingly losing his temper. The outbursts, which were unpredictable, might occur over petty incidents. Their children, seven-year-old Jessica and nine-year-old Craig, were intermittently fearful, angry, and oppositional. Their father overreacted to minor misbehaviors such as refusing to instantaneously comply with his requests or accidentally spilling or breaking something. These overreactions included angry outbursts during which he demanded more respect. He ridiculed and denigrated his kids when they did not perform to his satisfaction. He also threatened them with dire consequences and slapped them at least once a week. He had recently begun calling his children names such as airhead, pinhead, and lazy.

As Mr. Rand sat sullenly listening, his wife and I discussed the problem. Mrs. Rand explained that she understood that her husband's temper was related to his frustration over his job situation. Up until the last year he had been reasonable with the kids and rarely hit them or screamed at them.

I turned to Mr. Rand and asked him to explain what he thought was going on. He described himself as a hard-working middle manager in a large corporation. His company had been bought by a megaconglomerate, and after a year of insecurity, many of Mr. Rand's colleagues had been downsized (fired). During the year his new "path leader" (boss) had led his "self-directed workteam" (department) into a position of "empowerment" (responsibility without authority) in order to enhance the new corporate "vision" (making more money for stockholders). The result was that Mr. Rand, as part of the "changed," "lean and mean" (gutted) corporation was forced to "broaden" (take on additional responsibilities) his "base of skills" (the skills of fired employees) as part of a "horizontal promotion" (more work for the same pay). No wonder the poor man was stressed out. But was it appropriate to take it out on his family?

Mr. Rand admitted that he was losing it too often. But clinical interview and family history revealed the old story of transgenerational modeling. Mr. Rand's father had a bad temper. As a result, Mr. Rand tended to bottle up his anger in fear that he would become like his father. He said, "I know what it was like to grow up with screaming, threats, and constant fear of being hit. I really feel awful, but I don't know what to do. I just can't seem to control myself."

Helping Mr. Rand to control himself involved a variety of techniques. But unlike some other parents with whom I have worked, he had voluntarily agreed to come to therapy. It was clear that he was predisposed to deal with frustration by striking out within his family setting, where, as opposed to his work situation, he was in control.

I could help Mr. Rand in terms of his self-concept, his feelings about the threat of the loss of his job, and his fears of not being able to support his family. Of course, I could not guarantee that he would keep his job or that he would not face a lowered standard of living. But I could guarantee, if he followed my suggestions, that he could learn how to control his temper and stop using punitive, counterproductive disciplinary techniques. I helped him by using procedures I have developed over thirty years with angry, aggressive parents and spouses.

Eight Steps to Anger Control

Anger control, as I have formulated it, involves eight steps. These techniques were designed for families in stress and are rooted in research, clinical reports of other professionals, and my personal experiences as a therapist. I think most parents who are well motivated to change can master much or all of what I describe in this section without help from a therapist. However, if you are unable to master the techniques and feel that things stay the same or get worse, you may need to get help from a real live therapist who can provide objectivity and support that you can not get from a book. What follows are the eight stages to controlling your anger and brief examples of how I dealt with the Rand family to illustrate each point.

1. *Determine where you learned the style of your aggressive anger expression.* You can figure this out by analyzing your own family history. With Mr. Rand, it was quite clear both to him and to me that his father was the mediator in how he learned to handle his anger. If you go back as far as possible, perhaps to your great-grandparents, you may discover how each generation learned, through modeling, how to lose their tempers.

2. *Recognize that your aggressive behavior was learned and therefore it can be unlearned and replaced with new ways of expressing anger.* Once you have reviewed how you learned to express anger by aggression, you must now think of appropriate ways to express and deal with your own anger. Begin by accepting that anger in itself is not bad—and therefore you are not a bad person even if you get angry frequently. It is how you express it that becomes a problem. Once you shed your rationalizations, guilt, and other useless beliefs about anger, you will be able to get a handle on it.

By practicing, you can learn to recognize your anger and not deny it. Denial can result in the development of more anger and aggression as you try to rationalize your aggressive behavior.

You can begin by telling your family how you feel by using "I messages," which we already discussed. For instance, it is appropriate for Mr. Rand to say, "Craig, it really makes me angry when you hit your sister. You are bigger and stronger then she is, so it is not fair." Mr. Rand has told Craig how he feels and has described the misbehavior. Next, he must tell Craig the appropriate behavior by saying something like, "I know it gets you upset when she takes your toys, but when she does I want you to ask her for them. If she refuses to give them back to you, then you can tell me or Mom."

When Mr. Rand comes home from a bad day at work, instead of striking out at the kids or his wife for unrelated behavior, he should say, "Listen, gang, I really had a bad day at work. I need some time to myself so I don't lose my temper at you because I am angry at my boss."

3.   *Identify the triggers—the thoughts that lead to your aggressive behavior.* Anger control training depends on learning what thoughts immediately precede your aggressive actions. You can begin the process by thinking about the last time you were angry. After you visualize the whole scenario, think of what you thought or said to yourself before you began to lose it.

Mr. Rand described several recent events where he blew up at his children. I will give you one to illustrate what he had to recall and how I dealt with it.

ME: So last Wednesday, after dinner you were sitting in the family room watching television when you had a blowup with Craig. Tell me exactly what happened.

MR. RAND: Well, we had eaten dinner and my wife was cleaning up. I was wiped out and wanted to be left alone. Craig came in and asked if we could watch one of his shows together. I told him that I wanted to see the rest of what I was watching and suggested he watch his show in our bedroom, which has another TV set. He began to whine that he wanted to stay downstairs. I repeated my suggestion, and he claimed that I never wanted to spend any time with him. The more he whined, the more I got pissed off. Finally, I lost it. I started screaming at him that if he didn't leave me alone he would get a smack in the mouth for being such a whiner.

He started to cry, and at that point I grabbed him and dragged him to his bedroom, threw him in, and slammed the door.

ME: How did you feel afterward?

MR. RAND: Well, I was still angry for quite a while. I felt that I deserved some peace and quiet at the end of the day. Then when I calmed down, I realized that all Craig really wanted was to spend some time with me. But by then it was too late, so I kind of forgot about it and got ready for the next crisis in my life.

ME: What do you mean?

MR. RAND: Well, if it's not my kids, or some crisis with the house or the cars, something will surely occur the next day at work.

ME: So you feel that no matter where you turn there are problems.

MR. RAND: You got it.

ME: Good, we are making progress. Now, tell me, do you have a kind of general feeling of anxiety or vigilance? You know, the feeling that you better be ready for anything. Like a feeling of foreboding about what crises will occur each day?

MR. RAND: Right. Right. That is exactly it. I have this kind of general anxiety mixed with anger.

ME: Is that the feeling that helps to trigger your temper?

MR. RAND: Maybe, I don't know.

ME: Before we turn to what happened with you and Craig, let me ask you something very important. Do you lose your temper at work the way you do at home?

MR. RAND: Sometimes, but I have to keep it under control there. Although I do sometimes scream at one of my subordinates when they really screw up. But mostly I lose it with my kids and my wife.

ME: So even though you said that you inherited your temper, you were able to control it pretty well until recently. Also, even though you claim that you really can't control yourself, you generally do at work. Is that right?

MR. RAND: Yeah, I guess so.

ME: OK. That means that you are able to control your temper when it is in your best interest. That is, if you lost it often at work, especially if it was irrational, you could lose your job.

MR. RAND: Right. Right. I guess I do control it when I have to. But tell me why I completely lose it at home.

ME: OK. Let's find out the thoughts that trigger your actions when you are angry. You see, we all say something to ourselves as we feel emotions. Just before you started screaming at Craig for not leaving you alone, what thoughts, not feelings, came to your mind?

MR. RAND: I guess I had two thoughts. First, I thought, "Why doesn't he listen to me when I tell him something?" The second thought was something like, "Here we go again! I can't get control of things."

ME: Now think carefully of a few other times when you lost it with Craig or your daughter. Did you have similar thoughts?

Mr. Rand recalled that he usually had similar thoughts when he lost his temper at home. Especially recurrent was the thought that he didn't have control. Yet when this thought occurred at work, he was generally able to short-circuit the aggressive expression of his anger by saying something like "It's not worth it to lose my job over what this idiot said or did to me."

We discussed Mr. Rand's feeling of loss of control and his feelings of having no control over his own father's aggressive behavior. This discussion helped him gain more insight into the sources of his temper. I then helped him to realize that the trigger for his aggressive punitive actions at home was the thought, "Here we go again! I can't get control of things." The next step was to help him to not pull the trigger.

4. *Learn relaxation techniques*. There are many books, tapes, and training seminars devoted to relaxation training. The underlying theory is that when you get angry or anxious, your body goes into a mode in which fight-or-flight hormones are released, your muscles tense, and your body prepares for some type of action. Now, you can't go into this tense, ready-for-action mode unless your muscle system and your brain are "coiled" and on alert. Therefore, if you can interfere with one or the other, the system doesn't work.

Gurus, witch doctors, hypnotists, medical researchers, and psychologists have all discovered that when they induce relaxation, which is antithetical to anger, tension, and aggression, the latter states can not occur. Whether it is a guru teaching meditation, a witch doctor chanting, a hypnotist suggesting that you are relaxed, a physician giving you Valium, or a psychologist using a biofeedback machine to teach you to relax specific muscles, it is all basically the same principle.

This is how it works: You identify the trigger, then—once you've taught yourself to relax—you practice thinking the triggering thoughts and using your particular relaxation technique to counter the anger response instead of allowing it to take hold. Voilà! No aggressive response, no lost temper, no lousy discipline. Sound like magic? Step 5 gives you more detail on making it work in real life.

Where and how do you learn relaxation procedures? You could start with some commonsense prescriptions. My mom used to tell me, "When you start to lose your temper, count to ten and walk away." It took a doctoral degree and years of practice to make me realize that this was very sound advice, although I would add a little to it. Here is what you can do without taking a relaxation course.

Go to a quiet place and sit down in a chair or lie down flat on the floor or a bed with no pillows under your head. Place your hand over your diaphragm (the upper part of your stomach where it meets your rib cage). As you count ten slow deep breaths, concentrate on breathing from your diaphragm rather than your chest. When you are successful you will feel your stomach rather than your chest rising and falling, and you will begin to feel a relaxed sensation.

Deep breathing is the simplest way to obtain the relaxation response. Another technique is called deep muscle relaxation. Begin with the deep breathing. Then begin to relax each muscle group by visualizing or thinking about the muscles and saying to yourself that you are relaxing the muscle group. You can begin with your feet, go on to your calves, thighs, pelvic area, hands, forearms, shoulders, chest, jaw, and all your facial muscles. You pick the order and the best way for you to visualize how to relax.

Another procedure is imagery. Just start with the deep breathing. With eyes closed, imagine a peaceful, quiet, relaxed place you have been or seen or create in your mind. Just breathe slowly and deeply and focus on the scene anywhere from one to ten minutes.

These are some of the simplest procedures you can learn at home. However, if they don't work, you may want to see a psychologist who specializes in behavioral relaxation techniques, which could include teaching you self-hypnosis or using biofeedback or clinically standardized meditation. I have found that a combination of several techniques when used with the teaching of self-hypnosis is generally effective because with hypnosis you can teach yourself to relax when you say specific words or phrases.

5. *Learn to use the relaxation techniques when anger or aggression trigger thoughts occur.* Whichever technique or techniques you find effective, you should practice every day until you can voluntarily put yourself quickly into a relaxed state. Once this is accomplished, you are ready to use relaxation as a counter to aggression. Here is what you do.

First, practice by imagining a recent situation in which your child really pushed all your buttons. Try to remember the situation as if watching it replay on a video. When you get to the triggering thought, stop the tape and do your relaxation exercise. Keep practicing this and vary it in any way you find helpful.

Next, picture common disciplinary situations that you can anticipate. With Mr. Rand, once he learned the relaxation response, he pictured a number of situations that were likely to occur in the evening after work. He began to practice or rehearse in his imagination how he would use the relaxation response to defuse his anger. He found it most useful to practice right before he came home. His practice also involved the next two steps, which consist of self-dialogues designed to substitute rational for irrational beliefs, thoughts, and actions, thus producing effective rather than ineffective discipline.

6.   *Recognize the irrational basis for beliefs associated with aggressive parenting.* This usually involves a major change in beliefs and concepts of parenting or at least parental agreement to suspend aggressive acts like hitting, screaming, and making denigrating statements. I have discussed these throughout this book. With Mr. Rand, it was at first difficult to get him to associate his father's abusive spankings with his own "normal" smacks on the behind. Through discussion, "lectures" from me, and trials of other techniques, he finally agreed that spanking was a bad idea and stopped doing it. We substituted a behavioral program and family council meetings that helped tremendously.

7.   *Learn self-dialogues to prepare for confrontations.* Rehearse appropriate ways of expressing or explaining away angry feelings. Mr. Rand said things to himself like, "When Craig starts to whine, I know it is because I have not given him enough attention. Getting angry doesn't solve the problem."

Rational, true self-statements include "My anger only seems to lead to useless aggression—it just doesn't help" or "When I start to get angry I should begin to think of ways to express my anger appropriately rather than spasming out" or "It's not worth it to get angry—I just end up with a knot in my stomach." You can substitute whatever other symptoms you get for the last one—the principle is the same.

8.   *Learn to use effective, positive discipline techniques.* It is clear that when I ask people to give up hitting and screaming, I need to

give them other techniques. By the time you finish this book you will have reviewed the major techniques described in over eighty discipline training programs.

Now that we have talked about how to handle your anger, let us turn to your child's anger.

Understanding Your Child's Anger

It is normal, healthy, and expected that infants, children, and adolescents will at times feel anger as a result of frustrating circumstances. Frustrations in childhood are a part of life and are caused by common events such as delayed gratification, inability to achieve goals, and barriers that block communication with parents, siblings, and peers. So even though anger is a normal emotion in children (as in adults), learning how to control and express it appropriately is one of the most important developmental tasks related to discipline. Early patterns of anger expressed as aggression and hostility can portend lifelong problems. Therefore, as a parent, you must distinguish between developmentally appropriately expressed feelings of anger as opposed to inappropriate expressions such as physical or verbal aggression against others, destruction of property, and stealing. Also, you must distinguish between transient feelings of hostility as expressed in verbally aggressive statements such as "Mommy, I hate you" and "I wish I could kill my teacher" as opposed to real deep-seated and ongoing anger. Understanding expected behaviors at particular ages is an important aspect of differentiating transient anger from underlying hostility.

During most developmental stages, anger and some types of aggression may be expected in most children. For instance, conventional wisdom tells parents that before two years of age, their children may try biting and hitting the very hands that feed them. Between two and three, many children flirt with expressing their anger through temper tantrums. Adolescents may fly into rages when their needs for independence and autonomy are thwarted.

For instance, there is nothing more provocative to adolescents than last-minute parental demands that force them to give up planned activities with peers. If you really want to see your seventeen-year-old son go into orbit, promise him the use of the family car for a date with a "hot chick" and then, over some minor misbehavior, renege on the use of the car several hours before his date.

Situations like these may all occur as a function of normal developmental stages. Children's angry responses, although neither desired, pleasant, or necessarily needed, should be expected. Just don't overreact. For instance, what should you do when you tell six-year-old Stuart that he can't watch his favorite television show because he must go shopping with you and he has a fit and screams at you, "I hate you. I wish you were dead!"?

In most cases, six-year-olds don't fully comprehend the meaning of death. Further, unless you have a really disturbed relationship with your child, his response may have been inappropriate, but it is not the malevolent statement of a psychopathic parent-killer. But many parents would consider that Stuart was a horrible, selfish, mean child who didn't care a whit about his parents. If you understand these statements as representing a transient feeling of anger resulting from total frustration, you could respond, "I know that you are really angry at me, but you still have to go with me. I can't leave you at home by yourself, but when you come home you can watch another show."

In general, anger is self-limiting. That is, even if you respond inappropriately, a child's anger over transient frustrations will fade away. However, if anger-provoking interactions are part of a regular routine, you and your kid are in trouble. Hostility develops in children who are constantly frustrated, fearful, denigrated, or abused in any way. This situation may lead them to develop hostile and aggressive styles of interacting with others.

How to Produce Hostile Children

The following three parental syndromes, when they occur on a regular basis, are sure to cause children to become hostile. Because hostility is a major contributor to aggressive misbehaviors such as stealing, lying, fighting, and opposition to all rules, it is important to note these well.

The Hitler Syndrome. This parent always demands reflexive obedience, motivates almost exclusively by punishment, and has little or no empathy. Family life is governed by a set of immutable rules that have been carved in stone. Deviance invariably ends in punishment. The child learns these traits and identifies with his parent, the aggressor. No wonder this child becomes a bully, a cheat, and a sneak.

The Wimp Syndrome. This parent is the opposite of the Hitlerite. The wimp sets no limits, is fearful of any childhood expression of anger, and therefore always gives in to the child. Wimps want to be buddies with their children and are fearful that if they set limits, their children will be angry at them. As a result, the wimps' children expect the world on a platter, and when it is not served up, they spew forth aggression and destruction on those who dare to frustrate them.

The Perfectionist Syndrome. This parent is overly concerned with the child's accomplishments. The perfectionist is overdemanding, has little or no understanding of developmental limits on children's ability to perform, and conveys to children that they are only valued for their performance and achievements. Children of perfectionists may bottle up a lot of anger that can explode at themselves and others. They feel a deep and abiding sense of self-denigration.

Chronically hostile children may have intense feelings of inadequacy, rejection, and alienation. They may be distrustful, fearful, and generally angry toward family, school staff, or peers. They can develop severe pathology if they are victimized constantly by teasing, scapegoating, or perceived unfair discipline. They are often agitated, depressed, and prone to having homicidal and suicidal fantasies. For instance, they may fantasize killing their tormentors, thereby wreaking revenge, and then killing themselves to become martyrs.

Hostile children who have the triad of fire setting, cruelty to animals, and bed wetting past five or six years of age and are abused are at great risk of becoming delinquent and are in need of professional help. Other danger signs include consistent refusal to accept blame, responsibility for misbehaviors, or punishments. They are often obsessed with violent TV, weapons, losing face in front of peers, and revenge against those who have crossed them.

All of these behaviors are signs of problems that may require professional help. But the suggestions that I make here are similar to those I use in training professionals to work with hostile, aggressive children. They will certainly be useful and effective for normal childhood anger and aggression.

How to Defuse Your Child's Anger

Try to stay calm and objective. Remember that anger is self-limiting. This means that the body's ability to sustain anger is limited. Your child will eventually run out of the chemical fuels and emotional energy needed to sustain anger. Faced with an angry child, you don't have to worry about gaining control immediately as long as there is no threat to anyone or anything. To remain objective, force yourself to focus on your child's behavior rather than on how you feel.

Since anger is self-limiting, it's best to try to wait it out. This may seem easier said than done, so try these ten approaches to help you weather the storm:

- Use silence.
- Offer acceptance and recognition of your child's anger, frustration, and pain.
- Assure him that you will stay there and listen.
- Encourage her to tell her side of the story.
- Allow him to relate facts and feelings in his own way, even if he curses.

- Use empathetic and reflective listening.
- Allow and encourage her expression of feelings.
- Restate facts and feelings.
- Attempt to clarify statements of his perceptions of events.
- Encourage continued talking by giving leads and prompts such as "Go on, tell me more about it . . . so how did you feel when I said that . . . what upset you most?"

When your child calms down, then you can talk about possible consequences of the aggression. You can discuss alternatives to punishment such as doing something to make up for the aggressive behavior, apologizing, or analyzing why it happened and what to do to avoid inappropriate behavior the next time.

What Not to Do When Your Child Blows Up

When your child blows up, do not lose your temper over things such as obscene language. Likewise, do not unrealistically reassure the child by denying that a problem really exists. Do not become judgmental by saying who is right or wrong, or by defending someone else, contradicting, changing, or disagreeing with the child's perceptions of the topic or the situation. Don't lecture or advise about what must be done, or require justification for actions or feelings. Don't belittle, denigrate, or ridicule the child's perceptions or ideas, or raise your voice, crowd in too close, or use menacing behaviors such as clenched fists, posturing, or glaring.

Once things calm down you can talk about the underlying problems. Remember that aggression, whether verbal or physical, is the reaction to a host of possible underlying feelings including alienation ("You hate me" or "You think I am too much trouble to be in this family"), frustration ("Why couldn't you give me one cookie, I was really hungry?"), jealousy ("You love my sister more than you love me"), or failure ("You think I am stupid"). The anger and aggression indicate the child is unable to cope. You should minimize discussion of the behavior and focus on what triggered the aggression and what can be done to avoid it in the future. If the aggressive behavior or blowups are repeated, use the same techniques with the child that I described for parents to learn anger control.

When the child is calm, and if punishment seems necessary, explain to the child that you understand that punishment probably will not change the conditions that caused the child's anger. Even though you understand this, the child must learn that some misbehaviors require punishment at home just as they do in the real world. As soon as possible, talk the situation over with the rest of the family in a calm way and again focus on the conditions that caused the situation rather than on the immorality of aggression. Finally, remember that "to err is human; to forgive divine"—anger and aggression are expressions of frustration and pain.

But Suppose My Child Attacks Me or Refuses Time-Out?

Several years ago, I got a call from the *Sally Jessy Raphael Show*. They were planning to do a show about situations in which parents, in the name of discipline, cause serious and in some cases fatal harm to their children. They were also interested in what to do, instead of responding by hitting or beating, with children who really flip out and threaten to attack their parents. I suggested that I would be happy to demonstrate that no matter what, you don't have to hurt kids. I agreed to demonstrate techniques of physical restraint, but the caveat was that they must give me equal or even more time to talk about techniques of responding to and de-escalating children's anger.

When the show began, more than the first half was spent on a case in which a young child, I believe about six years old, died when he had a pharyngeal spasm as a result of his parent's washing his mouth with soap for his use of obscene words. By the time everyone recovered from hearing this tragic story (I was in tears) and heard several other speakers, they wanted to give me five minutes at the end of the show to demonstrate how to restrain children and if necessary take them down without harm. I came on stage at a commercial break and told Sally that I did not want to be remembered by millions of people as that guy who showed how to grab kids instead of killing them. I wanted time to talk about de-escalation and refused to demonstrate physical restraint. She was very gracious, and I ended up making a pitch against spanking, which I could do in five minutes.

I use this incident to illustrate my concerns about empowering parents with any techniques that have potential for harm. I realize that in the real world children do explode at times and you should know what to do when they end up attacking someone. There may be times when your frustrated and angry child may bite, hit, or kick you, or at least try to. Parents have the right and responsibility to assert themselves in such situations and to use force when necessary to protect themselves, others, or property, or to prevent children from self-injury. However, as you guessed, I do not believe counteraggression by the parent is very helpful.

Counteraggression makes things worse in the long run. Rather than hitting children, I train parents and teachers in techniques of therapeutic physical restraint. These procedures are only to be used in emergency situations when an attack has occurred or in very specific incidents such as refusal to comply with time-out. However, rather than laying hands on children, it is always preferable to allow for de-escalation of anger, as I have already described. While the use of force offers a quick short-term solution for dealing with aggression, especially if the goal is to minimize harm, experience shows that force tends to be used too soon and too often when it is available at all.

Physical Restraint

Physical restraint training is 90 percent de-escalation techniques and 10 percent physical methods such as the basket hold shown in Figure 7.1. This hold requires grasping children from behind by their wrists, forearms, or upper arms in a manner that their arms are crossed and locked. This technique allows you, assuming you are strong enough, to physically restrain and control children and prevents them from hurting themselves or you. There are also methods of take-downs and releases that you can use when the child grabs you. But these should be acquired from actual instruction—they're too complex to pick up from a book.

Let me illustrate an example in which restraint might be used. Toddlers sometimes begin to bite as a way of expressing their anger. I have seen too many cases where the adult response is to bite the child back, or if one child bites another, to have that child bite back. I heard of a case where the child was forced to bite himself. More frequently parents just smack the kid for biting. Yeah, good message: "You hurt me, but I am bigger so I will hurt you back!"

I recommend the following when a child—like eighteen-month-old Julie—wants some cookies and threatens to bite you:

FIGURE 7.1 Standing Basket Hold.

PARENT: Julie, I know you are angry, but I will not let you bite me.

JULIE: I want cookie.

PARENT: I will give you a cookie after supper.

Julie starts to grab your arm to bite you. If she does manage to bite, instead of pulling back—which may result in Julie coming away like a shark who has just ravaged a victim—push toward her and hold her nose so she can't breathe. This will cause her to let go. However, your first and best strategy would be to distract her by offering her a toy or starting to do something she likes. But even though distraction is often a successful ploy with toddlers, let's say it doesn't work in this case. You say, "If you don't stop you will have to sit in time-out for thirty seconds."

You could sit her in a chair for thirty seconds. But let's say she refuses that option and continues to try to bite. You now have two choices: hold her in time-out, or hold her in one place. In this instance, you decide she's too young to hold in time-out, and so you choose the latter. You say, "If you don't stop I am going to hold you in one place for one minute." (Julie does not really understand the passage of time involved in one minute, but it is good to use terms that will eventually have meaning.)

Julie continues with the attack. Do not let her bite you. If she does not desist, gently put her on the floor, face down, and hover over her on hands and knees without putting your weight on her. Despite her efforts, she can't escape from this circle of arms and legs. You say calmly, "Julie, biting hurts. I will not let you bite me or anyone else. I will let you up, but you can not bite me. If you try again, I will hold you in one place again."

If a child gets this kind of response every time, I have found the behavior generally stops in a few months at most. If it doesn't, there may be serious problems that require professional attention. But it is important to persist by being loving, kind but firm, and insistent.

Older children may sometimes refuse time-out. What should you do? My advice is to put them in a room. If they are really angry, they may scream, cry, kick the door, and possibly break things in the room. If the latter is the case, don't put them anywhere they can break things. This may necessitate holding the child in a time-out chair for the prescribed time.

Here is how to hold children in time-out. Sit in a low chair—the one you use for time-out if it is not too small—and hold the child in front of you with a gentle but firm basket hold. Be careful if the child struggles hard enough to risk injury. Holding by the upper arms will generally prevent this but if the child struggles too much, you are better off letting go but telling the child that he or she will have to go to time-out later. If you decide to hold on, either put your face against the child's back or lean back far enough so the child can not head-butt you. Wrap your legs around the child's legs so you do not get kicked. It is also possible to do a basket hold in an adult-sized chair with the child on your lap. Another version is to sit with your back to a wall. With legs spread you can keep the child in a basket hold. Figure 7.2 illustrates two versions of the seated basket hold.

Never use physical restraint unless you feel confident that you are strong enough. Use it only when you have already tried everything else, and do not use it if you can't stay calm and think out what you plan to do. Be careful if you are in a confined space or on a hard floor (where you are more likely to get hurt or to hurt your child), and calmly warn your child of the consequences of attacking you. When possible, attempt blocks and other avoidance techniques such as keeping furniture between you and the child trying to hit you, before engaging in a basket hold. Stay calm and talk to the child in a calming and reassuring way, saying that you intend no harm or pain and that you will be able to let go as soon as the child calms down.

Within the limitations of this book, I have given you an overview of how to handle normal and aggressive behavior. How-

FIGURE 7.2 Holding in Time-Out.

ever, do not confuse aggression with assertion. A child expressing healthy assertiveness should be dealt with entirely differently.

The Assertive Child

You tell ten-year-old Amanda and her eight-year-old sister, Fran, to get ready for bed. Amanda says, "Why do I have to go to bed at eight thirty? I'm older than Fran, and I should be able to stay up later. Besides, all of my friends go to bed at nine o'clock or nine thirty."

Which of the following scenarios might occur in your home:

DAD: Don't try to stall. You heard your Mom. Go upstairs and get ready for bed.

AMANDA: But I am not tired.

MOM: Stop arguing. It is time for bed, and that is it.

AMANDA: But it is not fair. I'm two years older than Fran. I should be able to at least stay up half an hour more.

DAD: You will do what we say. I will not stand for this disrespect and defiance. One more word and your behind will pay for what your mouth is doing right now.

AMANDA: OK. But this isn't fair.

In this scenario the parents asserted their will over the child by refusing to negotiate and then threatened a spanking. The child complied. Let's look at another way to approach this common problem.

DAD: Don't try to stall. You heard your Mom. Go upstairs and get ready for bed.

AMANDA: But I'm not tired. I'll just lie in bed until nine or nine thirty. You won't let me read or watch television, so I just toss and turn. Or if I do fall asleep, I get up an hour early.

MOM: Well, you know, Amanda, sometimes you do oversleep because you are not getting enough rest.

AMANDA: Yeah, but that is usually on Mondays when we have had such a busy weekend. Can't we compromise?

DAD: Well, it is true that you are almost always up in time, and you are older than your sister. What do you suggest?

AMANDA: What about if I go to bed around eight forty-five on Sundays and at nine fifteen during the week. If that works out I will try for nine-thirty.

MOM: That sounds reasonable, let's try it.

In this second scenario, Amanda was able to assert her rights as an older child. Nobody used power assertion to control anybody. The parents and Amanda used rational reasoning and were assertive about their views without resorting to threats. Assertive children learn through parental models to stand up for themselves by using rational arguments. Assertive parents use rational persuasion and teach children to respectfully negotiate so that the end result is a win-win situation. Assertion, as opposed to verbal and physical aggression, avoids techniques that harm or denigrate the other person. You can teach your children to respect themselves and the views of others by using many of the positive approaches we have already discussed. This will avoid the development of aggressive and hostile responses.

A special issue in terms of assertion involves handling physical or verbal attacks from others. Being assertive rather than aggressive does not mean that children should allow themselves to be beaten up by peers or older children. In the world of childhood or adolescence, negotiation and compromise are not always possible. Assertive children understand that no one has the right to hurt them. They know that it is OK to appeal to authority (parents, teachers, police) if they are threatened or actually hit or verbally abused by other children, teachers, or other adults. Also, they know they may defend themselves by hitting back if attacked.

I don't expect that by reading this chapter you will become an expert in dealing with anger and resentment—those most difficult of all emotions. But I hope that, with this distilled version of my thirty years of research, theory, and practice, I have provided you with the basic information you need. In the next chapter, I discuss techniques psychotherapists have found effective that you can adapt to use as parents.

8

Using Therapeutic Techniques

You should become familiar with the methods used by effective therapists to help patients solve problems, because you can use these same techniques to enhance and expand disciplinary procedures, reduce misbehavior, and develop high self-esteem in your children. Of the over eighty discipline training programs my colleagues and I have studied, almost all promote practical approaches that were originally developed and proven by psychotherapists. To begin to understand these techniques, most of which are used to improve interpersonal relationships, think of the qualities of your best friend—or the ones you would desire in a best friend. Good therapists, like good friends, are warm, caring, rational, good listeners, and supportive. Depending on orientation, most good therapists try to be nonjudgmental. These are also many of the qualities recommended for good parenting and effective discipline. Moreover, even therapists who may make value judgments about whether what the patient did was good or bad do not condemn the person. Instead, they focus on better solutions to the problems facing their clients. The same applies to effective discipline if you follow the rule that you should reject the misbehavior and not the child.

Seven Essential Qualities of Effective Psychotherapy

Successful psychotherapy usually requires that the relationship include mutual trust, a therapeutic alliance, and good rapport between patient and therapist. Also, the therapist must model appropriate behavior and problem-solving strategies. The patient must experience tension reduction, learn effective reality testing, and learn appropriate ways to express feelings.

Mutual Trust

Successful psychotherapists know that they must develop mutual trust with their patients. Even in situations that involve highly technical procedures such as biofeedback or hypnosis, failure is likely if there is a lack of trust and confidence between the parties.

Likewise, lack of mutual trust between adults and children undermines good discipline. For instance, you tell thirteen-year-old Steve that you can't take him to see a baseball game because of work commitments. Steve later finds out by accident that in reality you went out drinking with your buddies. Is it any different when Steve retaliates by smoking marijuana and swearing to you that he never even saw pot, let alone smoked it?

Therapeutic Alliance

In therapy, mutual trust leads to a *therapeutic alliance*, which in many ways resembles the process when employees, athletes, or friends strive in groups toward accomplishment of mutually accepted goals. These groups are most successful when all parties accept the goals and processes. This type of alliance is crucial to long-term, effective discipline. For example, behavioral contracts can only work when both adults and children agree on the ground rules, the types of rewards, and the timing for giving rewards. When contracts fail, it's generally either because they are unclear to some or all parties or because adults force the terms of the contract on the children.

As you will have noted at the beginning of this chapter, the qualities and techniques of effective therapists are not esoteric or mysterious. Many are reflected in the practices of good teachers and parents when they prevent and deal with misbehavior on a day-to-day basis. However, if your child's misbehavior begins to increase in intensity or starts to become chronic, you may want to focus on learning specific methods to address your child's problems.

Now don't say that I expect you to be a psychologist as well as a parent. My intention is to familiarize you with those procedures that have already been translated and proven successful for use by parents. I know that you are not a psychotherapist, and I know you can't be completely objective with your own children.

Recognizing appropriate boundaries between parent and child, you can be like a trusted friend, you can form a therapeutic alliance, and you can offer structure, guidance, and help in solving problems. I trust that after reading this book you will recognize when it is time to seek professional help.

Suggestion and persuasion are important elements in helping influence people to change. In a therapeutic alliance, children should not feel obliged to make immediate changes in their thoughts and actions, nor should they be subject to moral sanctions if they fail to do so. They need to be encouraged to internalize the reasons why they should change. Parental power and force cause only external changes that are short term. In a true alliance, both parties finally agree to behavior that is mutually acceptable.

Building Rapport

You must have good rapport with your child during normal times so you can cope effectively when the child misbehaves. Psychotherapists know that rapport is essential in forming a therapeutic alliance. The basis of rapport is mutual trust. To aid this process you need to convey to your children that you have "unconditional positive regard" for them. No matter what they do, they can tell you about it without fear of personal condemnation and rejection. I know I have said this repeatedly throughout this book, but that is because it is so important in parenting.

Good rapport is aided by conveying genuine feelings of interest, concern, and empathy. If you accomplish this, your child will feel that you are a consistent source of emotional support. A good way to establish rapport is to encourage your children, from an early age, to talk about problems they are having with their friends, their complaints about you, and their problems at school. Especially with young children, the complaints may sound trivial and boring, but you should have daily discussions about them anyway.

For instance, every day when you come home from work and before dinner, you could set aside ten or fifteen minutes to talk with your children about their day in school. Since I frequently encounter parents who miss the point about the long-term benefits of good rapport, let me begin with an example of the wrong way to approach the issue. You approach ten-year-old Jill, who is watching television late in the afternoon.

PARENT: Well, Jill, how was school today?

JILL: Fine.

PARENT: So nothing special happened?

JILL: Nope.

PARENT: OK. I guess I better start on supper.

Problem number one. You can not compete with the professionals who designed television shows to make your children into transfixed zombies. Forget it. You either have to turn the television off, wait for a commercial break and hope that the commercial does not distract your child, wait until a better time, or have a child who can watch television and talk to you at the same time.

Problem number two. Don't start with, "How was school today?" or any similar invitation to which the child can reply, "fine," "OK," or some other noncommittal remark. This is called a *convergent*, *or closed*, *question*—one that can be answered with one word. Instead, ask *divergent*, *or open*, *questions*. These require that the child describe, elaborate, or tell about something in detail. So instead of "How was school today?" you should say, "Tell me about what you did in school today."

If you only get a general response, probe with specific questions. For example:

PARENT: Well, Jill, how was school today?

JILL: Fine.

PARENT: What did you do in social studies?

JILL: Oh. We talked about the Civil War.

PARENT: What did you learn?

JILL: Mr. Jones showed us a map of Gettysburg and told us how the armies fought the battle.

PARENT: Tell me a little about it. (*Jill can talk about the battle. Once she starts talking, you can go on to other issues. For instance, let's assume that you know your daughter is having a problem with a classmate.*)

PARENT: What did you do with Jenny on the playground today? Did she still try to keep you from playing with Lana and Karen?

JILL: No. I think she knows, after I talked to her about it, that she really hurt my feelings. So today we all played box ball together at play time.

PARENT: So tell me how you felt about that.

JILL: Great. I'm glad you told me how to talk to Jenny about her being mean.

In this case, rapport was established by probing and asking questions to encourage discussion and clarify events and feelings.

Modeling

We have discussed modeling extensively, especially as a contributor to transgenerational parenting patterns. In psychotherapy, patients often idealize therapists and even consider them as parent figures. They tend to model their behavior on that of their therapists as best they can, so therapists know they must act rationally, calmly, and thoughtfully when dealing with all sorts of problems.

Children model their parents in very similar ways. I have already extensively discussed how transgenerational patterns of child rearing can cause the transmission of dysfunctional behaviors, but that's only half the story. Modeling works as well or better for *functional* behaviors. Children are much likelier to do what you do than to do what you say, so make every effort to model the calm and rational approach to the world you wish your kids would take.

Reducing Tension

Tension reduction occurs when your children feel that it is safe to express their innermost feelings, fears, and anxieties. Just talking about problems with a friend, confidant, or parent, even if there are no apparent solutions, helps to reduce tension.

Tension reduction is enhanced when you use active listening skills. Remember to reflect feelings and ideas, to try to be nonjudgmental, and especially to give the child ample time to talk. Tension reduction is obvious when you allow an angry child to blow off steam.

Many years ago, Bernard Guerney developed therapy techniques based on training parents to act as nonjudgmental, empathetic therapists. He called this Filial Therapy, on the assumption that most parents really can do therapy with their young children. Parents are trained by their therapist to use procedures promoted by Carl Rogers and adapted by Guerney. Rogers's Nondirective Therapy, or Client-Centered Therapy, consists of the skills of listening, reflecting, being nonjudgmental, and letting clients solve their problems without the direction of the therapist. The skills needed are the very same that I have promoted throughout this book. I will tell you the basics of Filial Therapy as I have used it with parents of children who are angry, depressed, or anxious.

First you must set up a regular time and place for your sessions. They should generally last half an hour to one hour depending on the child's age and attention span. They could be every day, twice a week, or once a week depending on the situation and your judgment. The therapy setting should include toys that are developmentally appropriate. For young children, these would include but not be limited to crayons, paints, dolls, doll houses, hand puppets, and simple board games. For older children the toys might include plastic blow-up figures that can be punched, model kits, and games like Monopoly.

The underlying goal is to provide a play arena in which children are free to express themselves and work out their problems. Once a regular time and place are arranged, you can say something like this to four-year-old Julia, who doesn't want to go to day care, "Julia, every Saturday morning you and I are going to spend time together playing. This is our special time. When we do this we will go to your playroom in the basement and close the door. No one can come in because this is our time. We will do whatever you want and you can say whatever you want during our special time. You are in charge."

This statement covers most of the ground rules. Older children may ask if they can use dirty words, since you have told them that they can say whatever they want. Or they might try to get you to give them things they shouldn't have, like violent toys or types of candy that you don't normally allow. Determine the limits by what you can tolerate and by common sense. In terms of freedom of speech, I recommend that children should be allowed to say anything they want during this time, with the understanding that they still don't have license to talk that way outside the sessions. As far as action goes, I recommend making it clear that they can't hit you or destroy valuable property, although they may break some of their own toys if that is their choice. The goal is that they feel free to express all of their emotions in ways that help them.

Let's see how the session with Julia might go. Although you hope that she will want to play school and act out her concerns about her day-care center, it is important that you allow her to determine when she is ready and allow her to take the lead in deciding what to play. Chances are, if she is troubled by something, it will come out during this time you spend together. Here is how it might work:

PARENT: Julia, what would you like to play?

JULIA: Let's play school.

PARENT: OK. You be the teacher, and I will be the child. Do you want to use these puppets?

JULIA: Yeah. (*They both put puppets on hands.*) Now I am the teacher, and you better go to sleep at rest time, Jane.

PARENT: Oh, teacher, what if I can't fall asleep?

JULIA: Then I am going to make you sit in time-out! (*Raising her voice.*) You can sleep just like all the good boys and girls. (*Scolding.*) You are a bad girl.

PARENT: I'm sorry, teacher, but I just can't sleep.

JULIA: Then you better lie quietly and not disturb the other children. If you move, you go to time-out.

You don't have to be a rocket scientist to see that Julia is having problems at day care around rest time. Without going into details, it is clear that the parent has discovered the problems, and that Julia sees her teacher as being very punitive. In the next scenario, Julia and her parent could reverse their roles.

Of course this brief introduction to Filial Therapy will not make you an expert. But if you are able to use the basic concepts of nonjudgmental listening, reflection of your child's feelings and ideas, and conveying unconditional positive regard, you should be successful with most common problems. Even if your child is not having problems, this is an excellent way to establish good rapport and a lifelong habit of effective communication with your child.

Testing Reality

Reality testing is the process by which patients learn to distinguish distorted beliefs, feelings, and perceptions from those that accurately reflect reality. For instance, ten-year-old Ralph might say, "The principal hates me. She picks on me whenever I am outside of class. Since she thinks I am bad all the time, I might as well do what I want in the hallway, the lavatory, and on the playground." Even though it may be true that the principal hates Ralph, it is likely that she is more concerned with preventing him from misbehaving than with catching him. Further, is it really true that she "picks on him" *every time* he is in the hall? That is unlikely. Finally, Ralph's reality is that he might as well misbehave, because she thinks he is bad anyway. The external reality is that he can avoid trouble by behaving for a sustained period, minimizing his time outside of class, and sticking close to the "good" kids, his teacher, or some other supervisor when out of class so that if the principal does pick on him it will be witnessed.

As a parent, you can help your child to face reality by doing all the positive and preventive things we have talked about in this book. Poor reality testing can result from overly punitive or overly permissive parenting. Once it is well established it is difficult to change. Unfortunately, a small percentage of children, especially those who are abused or neglected, have such poor reality testing that they require massive interventions. Here is an example of a boy who just could not test reality appropriately.

Frank, a fifteen-year-old oppositional and delinquent patient who was on probation with the courts for a number of defiant and abusive acts toward his single mother, was caught red-handed shoplifting in a mall. When I saw him several weeks later, he claimed that since the store got back the $200 worth of clothing, he was in the clear. When he didn't hear from the police for three weeks, he claimed, "They forgot about me."

When I pointed out that he was already on probation and that maybe I should find out his status, he said, "Don't call anybody. You will just get me in trouble. If you do, then they will remember what I did." I appealed to the other kids in his therapy group. They reiterated that the police and courts would not forget about him.

Despite our warnings, he now felt he was invulnerable and began a new round of hostile acts toward his mother. Needless to say, several weeks later the courts summoned him, and he was committed to a youth correctional center and other penalties because of both the stealing and problems with his mother. Frank's poor reality testing interfered with his ability to benefit from therapy. Although many of the other conditions of effective therapy were met, he just did not want to deal with reality. Why? Because his only discipline had consisted of spankings, beatings, and denigrating verbal attacks. He never learned rational problem solving.

Reality testing can occur in many ways. Sandy, a sixteen-year-old patient in one of my groups, constantly projected blame on others for everything bad that happened to her. Even when she was caught stealing, she blamed her friends who told her to steal. Also, she was unable to accept blame because she felt that the stealing was something that she had to do because she was a bad person, almost as if being a bad person was something outside of her that she could not control. When she finally began to understand that she was not an inherently bad person and that her stealing was related to her anger at others who constantly ridiculed her, she was ready to change.

Expressing Feelings Appropriately

Learning new skills, ideas, and how to deal with feelings is an important part of therapy. Patients learn to correct inappropriate or incorrect thinking and behavior about themselves and toward others. Depending on the orientation of the therapist, this may include such learning processes as talking about issues until the patient gains insight, practicing new interpersonal skills, or repeating new internal dialogues. Parents who use rational problem solving, moral persuasion, and modeling of appropriate behavior all provide children with the opportunities to learn new ways of solving problems. Chapter Seven offered an extensive discussion of appropriately expressing anger and resentment, so I will not discuss that here.

Children do not always do things that please us. In fact, there are times when our children's public displays or privately expressed thoughts may be disappointing or even downright disgusting. Therapists learn to deal with these feelings in an objective manner by avoiding judgmental attitudes and focusing on what these behaviors may mean. This takes a lot of tolerance, empathy, experience, and patience. If you need these qualities to make a living, they come much easier than if they are occasionally required for parenting.

Now if you are a candidate for the Parent Hall of Fame or have been nominated for parenting sainthood, you probably do not have to read this section. But if you are a normal parent like me, there have probably been times when your child's behavior has caused you to feel displeasure, disgust, and disappointment. As with anger, it is important for you to express these feelings in an appropriate way. As I have said many times, the most widely accepted guideline is to criticize the behavior, not the child. Let's consider an example of a situation in which parents might well be disgusted and embarrassed about their child's behavior.

Imagine that you have invited your employer's family to a somewhat formal dinner party. You have made sure that ten-year-old Billy is neatly groomed and well dressed, and have instructed him about how to behave. During dinner he begins to pick his nose and wipe the results of his mining efforts on the tablecloth. You notice that your boss's spouse has observed this as you are frantically (but as nonchalantly as possible) trying to get Billy's attention so you can stop him as you are carrying on a conversation with your boss. You think, "Oh, my God, it must look like I am raising a lout for a son. What did I do to deserve this revolting display?"

You are especially disgusted and disappointed because you know that Billy has been taught not to pick his nose, especially in public. You are embarrassed that your boss may have negative thoughts about you. You get up casually to go to the kitchen and ask Billy to help you. When you get into the kitchen, you are ready to smack the kid. Of course, you know that I think that is a stupid way to handle the situation, so let us assume that you launch a verbal attack instead of a physical attack. Not that I recommend hitting, but a verbal attack could do even more harm if it is typical of your method of responding to feelings of displeasure, disgust, or disappointment. Here is an example of what might happen and why it is wrong.

In the first scenario, you get Billy into the kitchen and say, "Billy, how could you be such a pig at the table. How many times have I told you not to pick your nose? You must really enjoy grossing people out and making me feel like a complete idiot who can't raise a son to be polite in company. Maybe you should go live in a pigpen—you certainly don't know how to live with civilized people."

Now, I am not a great defender of nose picking, nor do I believe that it is an inalienable right that should be defended by the ACLU. But give me a break. Was Billy really a p-i-g? Do you know for sure that he did it to gross people out or to make you feel like a complete idiot? Is Billy such a dirty, filthy child that he should really live with pigs? These and the other things you said were direct attacks on Billy's motives and character. If you say them enough, Billy will come to believe he is a pig and then you will wonder why he *always* acts like one.

A better response would be to use an "I" message and criticize the behavior. Here is how it might go. You say, "Billy, I felt very embarrassed when I saw you picking your nose. Do you need a handkerchief?"

Because Billy is not being attacked, he feels no need to defend himself. He knows that he should not have done it. He responds, "No, I'm OK. I am sorry you were embarrassed. I will try not to do it again."

Yes. I know you may feel that Billy's response is too good to be true. But if he really did not feel attacked and if he really was not trying to upset you, that is the way he might respond.

In this case, while criticizing the behavior, you offered an alternative behavior, using a handkerchief. In this case and in some examples I will offer, the focus is on separating the behavior from the child, which will help you to deal with your negative feelings effectively. Let me give you a few more right and wrong ways to handle common misbehaviors without either hitting the child or attacking the child's character.

- *Three-year-old Jane is playing with her genitals while taking a bath.*

Wrong: "Jane, stop that. You are a bad girl. You should not play with yourself there."

Right: "Jane, here is your rubber duckie—see, she goes quack, quack."

The parent knew that exploration of genitalia is normal in young children. Distraction can easily be used. If the child continues to do it obsessively and in a variety of situations, including in day care or in school, then there is problem. Unless there is a urinary infection or some other type of irritation, it may be assumed that the child is very unhappy and masturbates for pleasure and distraction from the unhappiness. It may require professional help to determine the cause.

- *Two-year-old Buddy dumps a big load in his diaper, and you don't notice it until the smell assaults you.*

Wrong: "Oh Buddy, you are such a bad boy. Look how dirty you are. Now I've got to change this stinky diaper."

Right: "Buddy, please try to remember to tell me when you have a poopy in your diaper. Then I can change it for you and give you a nice new diaper."

Is Buddy really a bad boy? Is he really a dirty boy? Of course not. Yes, his diaper is stinky, but he may have been too busy to notice it.

Never tell young children they are bad. Rather, tell them what they did that was wrong and then tell them what to do instead.

- *Ten-year-old Sylvia has been stealing money from home. Finally, although in denial because they can not believe their daughter is a thief, both parents realize what has been happening and set a trap to catch her. When she is caught she denies that she took the money.*

Wrong: "Sylvia, we know you took the money. That makes you no better than a thief. You are also a liar. What did we do to deserve a daughter who steals and lies? Haven't you learned anything is Sunday School about respect for your parents?"

Right: "Sylvia, we know you took the money. But what concerns us is why you took the money. Why didn't you just ask us if you needed more money?"

Of course Sylvia's parents were upset, just as any parent would be. But in the first case the parents denigrate Sylvia—they attack *her* instead of focusing on the behavior. They call her a thief and a liar. If they keep up that type of rhetoric, she will become a thief and a liar. However, in the second scenario the focus is on why she stole money. Children steal and lie for a variety of reasons. Sylvia may have used the money to buy things for peers in an effort to make friends. She may need the extra money because another child is extorting her lunch money. She could be stealing as a way of expressing her anger at her parents.

In the second scenario, Sylvia's parents focus on the behavior in an effort to understand why she did it. She knows that she shouldn't have done it, so giving her a lecture about Sunday School will not do any good. Also, her parents focused on alternative behavior when they asked her why she didn't come to them for money.

In all of these examples, it is clear that name calling and denigration do not begin to solve the problems of why the misbehaviors occurred. Instead, they are verbally abusive acts that make matters worse rather than better. This leads us to a brief discussion of the concept of emotional maltreatment and how to avoid it.

Understanding and Avoiding Emotional Maltreatment

Although it might seem like putting the cart before the horse, before I discuss emotional maltreatment much further, I would like you to do a brief exercise. By completing this exercise now, rather than after you finish this chapter, it might be easier for you to get honest, unbiased answers to my questions.

Sit down at a quiet time with paper and pencil. At the top of the paper list columns headed "father," "mother," and the names of your grandparents or other significant caregivers (teachers, coaches, and so on) and siblings. Under each heading, list all the negative phrases you can remember that each person used when criticizing you. Then, under each phrase, indicate the emotions you felt and actions you took when you were denigrated.

You may want to work on your list over some time. As you begin to remember incidents, others will pop into your mind. I must caution that if you were seriously emotionally maltreated, doing this exercise could cause the emergence of symptoms of posttraumatic stress disorder. These include recurrent and intrusive thoughts, memories, or dreams of the abuse or related incidents, feelings of anxiety related to the person or place where the maltreatment occurred so that you tend to avoid them, sleep disturbances, a heightened sense of vigilance, increased irritability and anger, or feelings of depression. If these occur, you should stop and seek help—they suggest you were a victim of emotional maltreatment.

Now spend some time thinking about when and how often you use those phrases yourself. Ask your kids and spouse to help. The main purpose of this exercise is to determine if you are doing to your children what was done to you. If you find that you are and you can associate how you felt when you were verbally assaulted, it will let you know how it must feel to your children. That will surely help you to stop. If you have real insight into this, you may be able to go cold turkey and stop on your own. Normally it will take some time, but you can do it on your own unless, as I said before, you are a survivor of abuse.

What Is Emotional Maltreatment?

Emotional maltreatment includes verbal assaults ("you are a slob"), putdowns ("you never do anything right"), ridicule ("you got it wrong again"), isolation ("you don't deserve to go on vacation with our family—so you will stay home alone") and rejection (always praising one sibling and making disparaging comments to the other). It also includes punitive sanctions ("you are grounded for five months for coming in late"), scapegoating ("I don't care if you didn't leave the dirty dishes on the sink this time, you are always doing things like that so I am punishing you for the times I did not catch you"), and sarcasm ("don't worry now about failing the final—you have been successfully failing all year"). Verbal maltreatment involves discipline and control techniques based on fear and intimidation. It tends to involve poor interaction between parents and children in which parents communicate a lack of interest, caring, and affection, and provide limited opportunities for children to develop competencies and feelings of self-worth. Parents who employ these techniques encourage children to be dependent and subservient, especially at ages when they are capable of making independent judgments, and also often deny them opportunities for healthy risk taking such as sports or dancing.

When parents continuously and inappropriately express their emotions to children in destructive ways, the children suffer a loss of feelings of safety, love, belonging, and esteem. Lack of trust in parents, as a result of constant denigration and criticism, can lead to anger, frustration, and alienation toward all authority figures. This combination is a frequent precursor to conduct problems.

I know of no research that documents the extent of emotional maltreatment by parents. But my students and I studied emotional maltreatment by educators and found that up to 50 percent of all students have at least one incident of the educator-induced emotional maltreatment that results in the student stress symptoms that may cause academic failure, alienation, aggression, anxiety, or depression. Because there is a reasonable possibility that your child may be exposed to emotional maltreatment in school and because this may trigger misbehavior, I thought I should give you a brief overview of what to do about it.

Emotional Maltreatment at School

In my book *Reading, Writing and the Hickory Stick* and in many documents from the NCSCPA, I spell out in greater detail what can be done if your child is a victim of either physical or emotional abuse in schools. You can use those resources if what I describe here doesn't work.

With the exception of some coaches of the Bobby Knight genre, who think that fear of ridicule and actual verbal abuse are motivating, few educators will openly defend psychological assault of students. Most school board policy manuals and teacher guides stress the importance of building self-esteem and promoting the dignity of each child.

The first indication that your child has been emotionally maltreated may not come from direct evidence—it's rare to get a first-hand look at maltreatment. Many parents who have called me said that they initially knew something was wrong because their children's behavior had changed. The usual response of young children who have been maltreated in school is withdrawal and crying; older children are more likely to react with anger and plans for escape or revenge.

For instance, a 1st-grader with a generally cheerful disposition began to cry easily, complain about going to school, and seem depressed. The parents assumed the child was just avoiding the more difficult schoolwork and tended to ignore the behavior. It wasn't until several months later that the parents discovered that the child was terrified of an unusually stern, punitive, and demanding teacher. The child had been severely scolded several times for innocuous misbehaviors such as whispering to a classmate. On one particular occasion she hadn't heard or understood the teacher's instructions for an assignment and was afraid to ask the teacher.

Also, she had heard other children being paddled. This child was usually well behaved and compliant and was either ashamed or afraid to tell her parents that she felt terrified of her teacher, whom her parents had praised.

Children's fear of reporting maltreatment by teachers is quite common. It is particularly common in families where parents have threatened children that they will be punished at home if they misbehave in school. Children can also develop it spontaneously, however, or by listening to classmates describe the reactions they encounter or expect at home.

If you discover the possibility of maltreatment of your child, you need to act quickly, rationally, and with clear goals. Even if you only hear about your child's classmates being abused in school, you should investigate. We know that witnessing abuse may be just as harmful as being a direct recipient. If one child is victimized, it is likely that others have been and will be affected, possibly your own child. There are too many schools in which educators, especially coaches, have long histories of physical and psychological maltreatment of students. Frequently, authorities are aware of the problems but refuse to act.

If you suspect your child has been maltreated, you should identify the maltreatment by writing out a careful description based on your observations of the child. Document the symptoms yourself, and with the help of a psychologist or other mental health professional, document the events surrounding the maltreatment by interviewing other children who witnessed it, clearly determine culpability (who is responsible), and decide on your goals and what you want to do next. It may be sufficient to obtain an apology from the offender, with assurance that the abuse will not recur. If so, a straightforward discussion may accomplish what you want. However, you should also consider whether the situation is serious enough to warrant filing an assault or harassment complaint with the police and obtaining a warrant for the teacher's arrest, filing child abuse charges, or obtaining an attorney and going to court. If you take any direct action the school may agree and discipline the offending educator. It is more likely that they will stonewall, deny, lie, and delay. If you take action against the teacher or school, it will generally not be easy to buck the establishment. You must be prepared to persist. Here are a few things you might want to know.

Mental injury was included in the Federal Child Abuse and Prevention and Treatment Act of 1974. In 1981, the National Center on Child Abuse and Neglect included the categories of verbal/emotional assault and passive and passive/aggressive inattention to needs in its description of psychological maltreatment. On November 20, 1989, the United Nations Convention on the Rights of the Child passed a series of resolutions that outlined an international agreement concerning the rights of children. Among the fifty-four articles passed, there are two that address a child's right to be free from psychological maltreatment. While the United States has not fully ratified the treaty, which has been approved by 187 countries, there is case law on emotional abuse that indicates that distress is a basis for civil litigation.

I have included this section on emotional maltreatment in schools because it provides a much-needed discussion of how children may be treated by educators who have not been trained to express their emotions appropriately. Now we turn to some specific techniques, derived from therapy, that you can use to help your children learn to think and act in appropriate and rational ways when faced with conflict.

Teaching Your Child to Think and Act Rationally and Appropriately

There are many books that present *affective* education techniques, that is, they focus on teaching students how to identify and appropriately express their feelings. We can't possibly cover all of these techniques here, but I can give you a few suggestions.

You can start with children at an early age by encouraging them to watch shows like *Sesame Street* and *Barney* that teach about expressing feelings appropriately. You can read them stories or fables or watch tapes that depict problems related to situations that can be resolved in a number of ways. Ask the child how the various people in the stories feel. Discuss the range of feelings and resulting behaviors that might be appropriate or inappropriate for a particular situation.

Now let us turn to some currently popular techniques derived from therapy that are promoted by many discipline training programs.

Learning Behavioral Self-Control

Behavioral self-control is a useful technique to help impulsive children. Psychologist Myrna Shure has developed an approach called I Can Problem Solve, which is especially geared to young, impulsive children. It can be used to teach any child how to think (not what to think) about how to solve typical interpersonal problems with peers and adults. Children are taught to generate a variety of possible solutions to deal with difficult interpersonal problems such as another child threatening them or taking away a toy. Children are encouraged to think about the possible consequences of each solution and then, after deciding which solution is best, develop a step-by-step plan to implement the chosen solution.

Maurice Elias and John Clabby developed a program called Social Decision Making. One goal is to teach children to calm down and reorganize themselves when they are in stressful situations that might cause them to blow up. They learn to understand social situations and the feelings of others in those situations. Like Shure, these authors teach children internal dialogues, or self-talk, in which they think about various strategies and their consequences. They learn to choose actions that are prosocial rather than antisocial.

When using self-talk for behavioral self-control, nine-year-old Johnny, who is very angry because he feels his teacher, Ms. Sloan, unfairly gave him a low test grade, is about to crumple up the test paper and throw it at her. But he thinks to himself,

"I am really angry and when I feel like this I always get in trouble. I better stay calm, take some deep breaths, count to ten and think of what to do . . . OK. Now I'm calmer. I would like to throw this at 'Ms. Slime' or spit in her face. But if I do either of those things, I will be sent to the office and maybe suspended. That will just cause me more problems. If I calm down and talk to her later, she may be fair, but if she blows me off, I will probably lose it. Maybe I should wait until I get home and show my parents why she was unfair. If I do that, they will probably help me, and even if they can't, at least I won't get into trouble. That is what I'll do. I will just smile at her, put my paper in my book bag and talk about it with Mom and Dad after supper."

Johnny has learned to recognize when he is angry and likely to blow up. He has also learned how to calm down and think of possible solutions and consequences. This lets him choose a plan and follow it.

Learning Social Skills

Social skills training involves actual practice of new skills or ones the child has not developed at the appropriate age. For instance, schools assume that by 1st grade most children will know how to share and be able to use that skill. If the child has not learned to share as a normal part of development, the child must be taught.

While most children learn social skills as they grow, some do not. Some do not have a clue about starting and sustaining a conversation, playing cooperatively, reacting to rejection appropriately, dealing with peer ridicule, and controlling their own aggressive impulses. Children who learn these skills begin to feel better about themselves.

For example, let's apply social skills training to seven-year-old Jane, who is rather shy and has not developed the skills to make friends. Normally, you might not think of a shy child as a potential discipline problem. But shy children, who may have low self-esteem, are at risk. For instance, they may be unduly susceptible to peer pressure to misbehave or they may eventually become hostile and avoidant because of ridicule or perceived rejection. Or in early adolescence they may turn to substance abuse to feel comfortable during parties or in preparation for social events.

When Jane perceives she is being rejected, she quickly withdraws and gives up. If you were shy as a child or have thought about the difficulties of being shy, you can teach her the skills she will need to be successful in school and work.

You can start by giving Jane feedback, in an unemotional manner, about a situation you observed when Jane should have been more assertive. This will help Jane to objectively understand what happened. You can have her tell her version and then tell her what you saw if you think she is distorting what happened. You should ask her how she felt and how she thought the others felt and her perception of their motivations.

Next, offer instruction in skills needed to be more assertive and outgoing. Help Jane to "target" specific behaviors such as initiating and sustaining conversations, offering to help others, asking for help, and observing actions and interests of extroverted children. Give her instruction in dealing with rejection. It's especially useful to explain that most times the rejection she feels won't be because there is something wrong with her, but because she has not properly identified all of the specifics in the situation. For instance, if she is rejected when trying to join a clique of girls on the playground, she might try to make friends with other children who are not part of an existing clique.

You should also model appropriate behaviors for making new friends. To help, you can have Jane read books or watch videotapes in which new kids make friends. She can thereby observe the appropriate behaviors in action.

The old reliable role-playing technique will help, too—you can take the part of another child while Jane plays her normal role. Then you switch, and Jane plays the part of the other child. This will help her to understand the nature of the interactions. The two of you may develop a checklist of things she should do to make new friends.

Once Jane understands the specific skills she needs, she can practice them with you. She can also, in her mind, rehearse how she will act in real life. She can also role-play with siblings, cousins, or other children with whom she is comfortable. She can try to identify a variety of situations she might encounter. Then, after sufficient practice, she can attempt to make friends by trying out her new skills in a real-life situation.

At this last stage, she must, on her own, begin to use her new skills in various situations. After each encounter, she can report back to you and discuss what happened. You can analyze the situation together and share in her success and alter her techniques if they don't work.

When Jane is able to use the new skills on her own, she will have achieved the major goal of social skills training, which is to internalize the skills learned. Then she can generalize the skills to any situation requiring them.

The same approach can work with much older children. For instance, seventeen-year-old Rick wants to avoid drinking beer at parties. Most of his friends are binge drinkers, and many routinely pass out at parties. He must learn refusal skills that will generalize to all situations in which he is offered or pressured to use alcohol or any other drug. He can develop his own refusal skills by practicing with his parents. He can find out how they refuse things they don't want to do. They can make a list of things he can say to refuse beer at a party. Then he can try them at the next party. The following example illustrates the point:

BILL: Come on, Rick, let's really get smashed.

RICK: Boy, Bill, you look like you are feeling no pain.

BILL: You got it, Ricky boy. Come on now, chug one down with me.

RICK: Hey man, I am really glad you are having a good time. But I just don't feel like getting smashed tonight.

BILL: OK. Be a party pooper. See if I care.

RICK: (*Puts his arm around Bill.*) Hey man, that's OK. You are still my buddy. I'll stay cool so I can look out for you if you pass out.

BILL: Thanks, buddy. See you later.

Rick can develop a host of other strategies. For instance, he can take on the role of designated driver. He can carry around a beer can with soda in it at a party. He can drink just one beer that he makes last all night. He can say he doesn't like booze any more because he hates getting sick or that he is having a great time without getting drunk out of his gourd. He and his parents can list all of the situations in which refusal skills might be needed and how the skills might be modified for certain situations.

Social skills training can help children to deal with their own behaviors. A similar approach can be used to help both parents and children prevent the misbehavior of others.

Learning Conflict Resolution

Mediation and conflict resolution techniques have roots in both hospital-based de-escalation procedures and the "peace and justice" era of the 1960s. Children can be taught de-escalation procedures to resolve problems without fighting. These are especially helpful with siblings who are constantly at each other's throats. Conflicts may be resolved with the parent as mediator. The ultimate goal is for children to learn the techniques of conflict resolution so they don't need a mediator.

If you act as a mediator, you must be nonjudgmental, refuse to take sides, and explain the ground rules. These include agreement that the person first making a complaint can talk first. The complainant is allowed to explain what seems to have happened. Everyone agrees to wait for his or her turn to talk. You can ask questions to clarify and summarize the discussion and provide an objective perception of the situation.

At the beginning, all kids must agree to respect each other's right to talk. There will be no interrupting, name calling, putdowns, threats, or fighting. Everyone will try to peacefully resolve the dispute. Once you understand the situation, disputants should be encouraged to question and talk with each other, try to figure what caused the problem, and attempt to come to a compromise solution. If necessary, disputants can make a contract of agreement regarding the causes and solution to the problem. Everyone should sign the agreement, which should be written in easy-to-understand, very specific language.

Good mediation requires all of the skills of good therapists that we have discussed. If you are an effective mediator, you will ask questions, reflect feelings and ideas, restate things that are not clear, summarize information, and help the kids to work on one issue at a time. If there are discrepancies, try to elicit the truth.

Who Is in Control? Beyond Conflict Resolution

Sometimes the normal skills of conflict resolution are not sufficient to mediate problems within families. This is especially true when parents and children are caught up in an unending cycle of misbehavior and punishment. Often punishers do not understand how their actions may exacerbate misbehavior. Consider the following case.

Mr. and Mrs. Landers called me in desperation. Their twelve-year-old son, Kyle, was totally out of control. Besides failing in school, setting a few fires, and frequent oppositional behavior, he constantly demonstrated his extensive repertoire of obscene words. As it turned out, the situation was not quite as dire as they described on the phone. Let me share with you a small part of the family interview and show you how children who appear to be victims are actually in control. We will enter the interview after I have gathered most of the information and I have discovered that both parents spank, smack, or whip Kyle with a belt at least once or twice a week.

ME: So, Kyle really gets you upset. Tell me what kind of behavior most frequently causes you to hit him.

MRS. LANDERS: Kyle has a foul mouth. I absolutely can't stand his constant use of the F word. He seems to use it at least a hundred times a day.

ME: Do you hit him every time he uses the word?

MRS. LANDERS: Are you kidding? I'd be arrested for child abuse if I did that. But when I ask him to do something and he tells me to "fuck off" or says, "fuck you," I can't stand it. That's when I really smack him.

MR. LANDERS: Yeah, I do the same. This kid has no respect.

ME: Now tell me something. When he says those things to you, does he know he's going to get hit?

MR. LANDERS: I guess he does. Although I can't say I hit him every time. But, I guess 90 percent of the time, he gets smacked by either of us when he does that.

From this conversation, it was clear that Kyle was in control. He knew that certain behavior would end up in him getting hit. I told the couple that it appeared to me that for some reason, Kyle wanted to be hit. They were incredulous and reluctant to accept that their son—who had a high IQ—would be so stupid as to invite the pain that they inflicted upon him. I scheduled the next session for Kyle, and it went something like this.

ME: So, tell me, Kyle. When you tell your parents to fuck off, do you know you are going to be hit?

KYLE: Yeah, I guess so. But they don't always hit me.

ME: So, in other words, you want to be hit. You must like pain.

KYLE: What do you think I am—crazy? I don't like pain.

ME: Well, let me see if I have this right. In your own words, you have told me that you know you will be hit most of the time when you do that. You have also told me that when you are hit, especially by your father, it is painful. So the way I see it is, before you tell them off, you know you are going to be hit, and you know it may be painful. In other words, you are planning to be hurt. So, what's going on?

KYLE: You want to know the truth? I don't care how much they hurt me. I just do it to make a point.

ME: What's the point?

KYLE: The point is that no matter how much they hurt me, they can't make me do anything I don't want to do.

When I held the first full family session, I reviewed what I had discovered. I explained that Kyle was in control, but I let Kyle tell his parents why he was in control. They were at first dumbfounded to discover that all the spankings they had administered for the last several years only served to perpetuate Kyle's behavior. While they realized the spanking was not working, they found it difficult to believe how much they had been manipulated.

The key to this mediation between parent and child is to first understand why the child exhibits behavior that is constantly punished. Once this can be revealed with the parents and the child present, the therapist can mediate other ways to approach the misbehavior. I have also used this technique successfully to deal with fighting among siblings. Take the case of ten-year-old Joe and his younger brother, eight-year-old Jim.

These two brothers were constantly fighting. The most common scenario was one in which Jim provoked his older brother by taking his toys, whining to their parents that Joe was dominating the television, or insisting that he be included in play activities with Joe's friends. Jim would often nag, whine, and cry until Joe either

202 THE CASE AGAINST SPANKING

gave in or beat him up. In the latter case Jim complained to his parents, and Joe was invariably punished. In mediation I pointed out to Joe that Jim was really in charge. I went through the scenario, and Jim admitted that he knew his brother would be punished but it was the only way he could think of to get what he wanted. When it dawned on Joe that he was being manipulated, he was furious. I also pointed out to Jim that he must like to be beaten up. When both realized how foolish their roles were, I was able to mediate and help them to develop a written contract that included a great deal of compromise.

You may be able to use most of the techniques I have described here without much more help. The basic principles are not complicated, and many are ones you use on a daily basis for problem solving. However, for more in-depth training, you could contact your local school psychologist—many schools now give training in conflict resolution and mediation.

Keep in mind that I do not expect that you will become a perfect disciplinarian by having read what I have told you so far in this book. But I think that by now you probably know the basics as well as anyone. Unless you have really serious discipline problems, my hunch is that you have a pretty good idea of what to do with the normal range of misbehaviors. If you want to become expert in the specifics of various techniques I've described, you can refer to the specialized books I mention in the Resources and Further Reading section at the end.

And finally, now that I have made a case against spanking and offered a full range of alternatives, it's time to consider a radical idea. . . .

9

What We Need to Do Next

- "Some kids need a good swift kick in the pants."
- "I need to hit my kids to get their attention."
- "If we don't have corporal punishment as a last resort in schools, kids won't have anything to fear, and they won't behave."
- "I was spanked when I was a kid and look where I am now."
- "The Bible says, 'if you spare the rod, you will spoil the child.'"
- "A good smacking is the only thing some kids understand."

I know that you have heard all of these before, but now, I hope, you know better than to believe them. I think I have made the case against spanking, without force-feeding you tons of psychobabble. For the sake of readability and brevity, I have left out many additional facts, figures, and statistics about why hitting is such a bad idea. I did this so that the bulk of this book could be devoted to information you can use right now to prevent misbehavior and design effective methods of discipline for your children. Not only do you have the facts to counter those who support inflicting pain on children, you know about the many alternatives.

Now that you know all this, what should you do? Well, at one level, I hope this book will help you to be a more effective parent or teacher to the children in your care. But I would also like to enlist your help in advocating to make a real dent in child abuse in America. Because I believe that if we all gave up the idea that hitting children is acceptable or necessary, we could reduce child abuse significantly in two generations. In addition, parents and teachers would be more open to learning about effective nonpunitive disciplinary techniques. The result would be fewer children with low self-esteem caused by ineffective and denigrating verbal and physical assaults.

If you accept the assignment to help reduce child abuse in schools and homes and to improve the discipline of American children, there are some additional things you should know. I will discuss them in this last chapter. You need to know a little more about the strong religious roots of spanking and how to respond, why policymakers are afraid to bring up the issue of a "no spanking America," how other nonspanking Western democracies are dealing with this, and finally what to do.

The Religious Roots of Our Punitiveness

By now it is clear that I believe that the source of our punitiveness is a cluster of beliefs nurtured and preserved through the centuries by the religious right. These beliefs are supported politically by the authoritarian right, shared by many moderates, and perpetuated by the media. They are rooted in the assumption that punishment is the best deterrent and treatment for misbehavior and crime. The religious and political right's ideology is the contemporary version of the Puritan obsession with punishment. The justification for inflicting physical pain on children lies deeply embedded in religion and tradition, as do the rationales for wife beating and brutal penalties for sailors and prisoners who resist authority.

Fundamentalists are among the most outspoken defenders of physical punishment, but they write and say what many others believe and practice. No part of America is exempt from the lure of punishment, and few are fully aware of its psychological consequences.

The problem of the religious roots of support for hitting kids is exacerbated by theologians who go far afield in searching for rationales for corporal punishment. For instance, Andy Osborne, one of my doctoral students, did a national survey of the beliefs and practices of religious leaders of many faiths. One of his research questions concerned texts and text passages that theologians used to promote the use of corporal punishment to their congregations.

Not surprisingly, many found their rationale in the Old Testament. For instance, the most popular punishment texts included Proverbs 13:24, "He who spares his rod hates his son, but he who loves him disciplines him diligently"; Proverbs 23:13–14, "Do not hold back discipline from the child, although you beat him with the rod, he will not die. You shall beat him with the rod, and deliver his soul from evil"; and Proverbs 22:15, "Foolishness is bound up in the heart of a child: the rod of discipline will remove it far from him."

Now, you will note that all of these are from Proverbs, ascribed to Solomon. But Solomon was a lousy father to most of the children he sired with his many wives and concubines. Further, his admonitions to not spare the rod turned out badly for his son Rehoboam, who lost a civil war. Rehoboam, taking counsel from young men who were brought up with him (we assume with no sparing of the rod either) regarding how to respond to the citizens who requested that he lift the yoke of oppression that Solomon had placed on them, said, "My father chastised you with whips, but I will chastise you with scorpions." This is an early lesson that violence breeds violence.

It is not surprising that many theologians have used Solomon as their guide for discipline, even though he at one time worshiped Moloch, the god who required infant sacrifices. But it is hard to understand how some of the Biblical sources used to support corporal punishment come into play—they do not even mention corporal punishment. For instance, some theologians used Proverbs 19:18, "Discipline your son while there is hope, and do not desire his death." Even more surprising was the use of New Testament sources to support the use of corporal punishment.

New Testament Compassion

Nowhere in the New Testament does Jesus Christ suggest the use of violence against children or adults. In fact, it seems clear that he was absolutely against the use of violence as a solution to problems in all situations. When the elders wanted to stone an adulterous woman he said, "Let whoever is without sin cast the first stone" (John 8:7).

Rev. Theodore Lorah of the Maple Grove United Methodist Church in Hunlock Creek, Pennsylvania, sent me his response to misguided theological support for corporal punishment. He suggested, "A better passage on raising children is found in Ephesians 6:1–4. Children are told to obey their parents, for it is right. But parents (fathers, specifically) are told not to provoke their children to anger, but to bring them up in the 'discipleship' and instruction of the Lord. Even the use of the word 'discipline' in place of 'punishment' is more to the point. Jesus took our punishment on the cross. We teach people to be disciples, followers; we don't punish. Disciplining is not accomplished by beatings."

The Singapore Syndrome

Most of us are aware that increasing trade and travel between the United States and Asia results in the rapid exchange of knowledge. This is accompanied by inevitable clashes of ideas between governments and citizens of Western and Asian countries over political, social, economic, and educational ideology. Differing concepts of discipline, crime, and punishment may erupt into national debates when citizens of each culture live and work in each other's nations. Such a clash occurred as a result of reactions to the proposed public flogging of an American teenager who was living in Singapore. The debate quickly rose to the diplomatic level when President Clinton publicly criticized Singapore's government. It also led to an uncritical acceptance of an ideology that is the antithesis of our democratic ideals. I call this cross-cultural transmission the Singapore Syndrome. Let me explain.

The frequent intercourse between Asians and Americans that results in the exchange and adoption of new ideas for each culture is a social phenomenon that may benefit both cultures when positive values and concepts are fostered. What I have labeled the Singapore Syndrome, however, is an example of a cross-cultural exchange gone awry.

The Michael Fay Case

Right-wing politicians are particularly susceptible to the Singapore Syndrome. Through careful demographic and historical research, I was able to trace the initial spread of this phenomenon to our shores. Orange County Assemblyman Mickey Conroy of the California Legislature appeared to be the first victim of the distorted thinking characteristic of the Singapore Syndrome, starting soon after he read about the proposed flogging—with a rattan cane dipped in salt brine—of eighteen-year-old Michael Fay. Fay allegedly confessed to vandalism and was sentenced to four months in prison, a $2,220 fine, and six lashes with a cane on his buttocks.

The sentence resulted in a media frenzy that lasted until several weeks after the reduced punishment of four strokes of the cane. As the facts of the case emerged, there ensued a national brouhaha over the issue of adolescent misbehavior and delinquency. Support for justice, Singapore style, was especially strong from the basically conservative audiences of most talk shows. I know, because I was a guest on many shows during that period. Also, with the help of several volunteers, I was able to collect an extensive file of clippings on the case. Before turning to Conroy, and others of his ilk, let me give you some background, accompanied by personal experiences.

In April 1994, I received a call from a journalist who was preparing an article for *Newsweek* on the flogging sentence. At that time the public knew little else than that Fay was convicted of the offense of spray painting several luxury cars, throwing eggs at others, and retaining Singapore road signs and flags that were given to him by friends as a farewell gift.

The journalist began the interview by stating that he had just received the results of an April 8 poll in which respondents were told, "A young American in Singapore is to receive a severe caning under the law there for punishing vandalism. Do you approve or disapprove?" My immediate response was "Don't tell me the results, let me guess. I bet that between 30 percent and 40 percent approved."

The poll showed that 38 percent approved and 52 percent disapproved of a practice that has long been banned in America. Now how did I know that? Well, after watching and conducting polls related to issues of youth misbehavior and crime and punishment, I knew that almost always between 30 percent and 40 percent of the public strongly support punitive policies as the most effective deterrent for social deviance and nonconformity. This is a result of the politics of punitiveness, a historical practice in which uncritical media and conservative politicians scare the public with inflated figures and exaggerated claims about lawlessness in America. Our most deeply rooted fears and yearnings about youth misbehavior were exposed as a result of the saga of Michael Fay.

How the Singapore Syndrome Spread

Soon after the story broke, the first victim of the Singapore Syndrome—Mickey Conroy—made national headlines. He idealized Singapore for the success of its toughness with criminals, the cleanliness of its streets, its no-nonsense justice system, and its low crime rate. If only we could be like Singapore! He proposed that juveniles convicted of vandalism get up to ten whacks with a wooden paddle. He said, "My goal is to humble these punks early on so we don't see them later in courts as murderers." Following this the syndrome spread to the heartland.

In St. Louis, Alderman Freeman Bosley made a similar proposal and bragged that he had been whipped plenty by his mother and that he had put the strap to his son—who at the time of the interview was the mayor. It wasn't long before the syndrome spread to the Atlantic coast states.

In North Carolina, Lawrence Graves, Guilford County candidate for sheriff, lauded the efficacy of caning and promised to give away a hundred canes for disciplining children. Meanwhile, the Florida legislature—taking time out from such important matters as trying to make it a crime to slander Florida fruits and vegetables, disemboweling regulations to preserve the fragile Florida ecology so as to promote more inane growth, telling educators what to teach and how to pray, castrating rapists, and dismembering the department of health and rehabilitation—received national attention for its desire to give ownership of children back to abusive parents.

Much to the horror of every national professional organization devoted to the welfare of children, Florida politicians passed legislation to assure parents that they could beat away on their kids without worrying about those pesky child abuse investigators. Governor Chiles refused to sign the bill, which would have sent abuse rates in Florida into the stratosphere, to be shared with the state's murder and incarceration rates. Senator James Hargett, a clear victim of the Singapore Syndrome and sponsor of the bill guaranteeing parents' "rights," was supported by another victim. Representative Berly Burke, whom I debated on *Oprah*, helped write the bill and became a defender of it to the national media. She was quoted as saying, "Bruises, welts, and broken bones do not constitute child abuse," and "We need to get tougher to reduce crime." Her distorted thinking caused her to ignore the extensive research showing that most violent delinquents and adults got that way from beatings by parents and authorities.

In debating with people like Burke, I am always astounded that they will go on national TV with little or no research; background in education, criminology, or psychology; or knowledge of the literature on discipline and tout themselves as experts. But that is an example of how extreme ideology distorts thinking and nourishes one's belief systems. As with most "spare the rod" clones, her wisdom about child discipline is based on a few passages in the Old Testament and her own experiences of being hit.

Is Singapore Crime Free?

A brief examination of supposedly crime free, squeaky clean Singapore tells another story. According to Francis T. Seow, former solicitor general and president of the Law Society of Singapore, the Punishment for Vandalism Act was passed in 1966 to stem the rampant political graffiti used by opposition parties. The graffiti stopped, but this must have made a significant dent in the message of the opposition getting to the public. Caning was then gradually added as a punishment for a variety of crimes, such as entering Singapore without a visa. The Singapore government believes that concepts of human rights promoted by Western democracies clash with Confucian ideals of order and obedience to authority. It has heavy fines for such horrendous crimes as chewing gum, failure to flush public toilets, public spitting, and feeding birds.

Despite Singapore's claim to law and order, the 3,244 canings in 1993 suggest that not everyone obeyed its laws that year—and evidence suggests that canings increase each year. True, when compared with American big cities, Singapore has a low crime rate (including homicides). But it also has stringent laws against gun ownership and almost no unemployment. And if it is so crime free, why does it have higher proportional murder rates than Australia and South Korea? Why are all of its crime rates greater than those in Japan, which is also an urban Asian country? Despite the death penalty for even low-level drug offenses, it still arrests people on drug charges each year (fifty-four in the first three months of 1992).

Our State Department's reports on human rights depict Singapore as a country that allows indefinite confinement, arbitrary arrest, police use of torture to obtain confessions, warrantless searches, restriction of political opposition and criticism, and control of foreign media. Unless you are suffering from the Singapore Syndrome, I doubt that this is the kind of government you want to rule you.

What Were California Legislators Thinking?

So why am I spending so much time discussing Singapore? I want to drive home the lesson of the slippery slope. Some American politicians, supported by a large minority of the population, think Singapore provides a model for discipline and punishment. We are already too complacent about the abuse of children in our own country. Many don't seem to realize that once you accept that any type of hitting by authorities is acceptable, there is no way of knowing where that will take you on the slippery slope to abuse and torture of adults as well as children in the name of discipline and law and order. I have already attested to the abuses in our own country, a land that believes in due process and other concepts of justice.

It is scary to me that Mickey Conroy, an American legislator, was able to muster enough support in the California House of Representatives in 1996 to consider legislation, which the governor had promised to sign, that would have permitted paddling of youths convicted of graffiti and would have introduced into the judicial system the beginning of the kinds of abuses I have documented in schools and homes. Conroy's fascination with hitting was shared by those who sponsored a companion bill to reinstate corporal punishment in schools.

In January 1996, I received a frantic call from Karen Jones-Mason of Legal Services for Children, located in San Francisco. At the time, almost everyone predicted that Conroy's bills would pass in the California Assembly. In response to her fears and request for help, I sent her pictures of the battered behinds of children who had been legally paddled in schools. In many of these cases, no actions had been taken by authorities—and even in the ones that went to court, many of the plaintiffs lost. She had these pictures blown up and used in a public hearing on the bills. Conroy and others claimed that they weren't talking about this kind of paddling, because it was obviously abuse. Advocates made it quite clear to the media and moderate Republicans just what slope they were starting down. The moderates headed for the hills rather than being per-ceived as supporters of official abuse. Conroy lost his needed sup-port from the Republican party, which will probably not touch corporal punishment for quite a while.

The pictures viewed by the legislators included one of the paddle-battered buttocks of a Georgia schoolboy. Even though pictures of his bruised behind didn't convince the Georgia Court of Appeals that it was abuse, they did help save California youth from a similar fate. Both bills were defeated. However, the most troubling aspect of this episode is that in the California Assembly, nineteen out of eighty legislators voted for AB 101, which would have allowed pad-dling back into the schools, and twenty-eight out of seventy-one voted for AB 7, which would have required paddling of children in court in front of the jury if they were convicted of graffiti offenses.

Ban All Spanking in America?

As I mentioned previously, I field-tested early drafts of this book with some friends who are also parents. Sandy, a very intelligent, loving, and supportive mother in her early thirties, has two young children. When I asked her to read a draft of my book, she told me that she did not believe in spanking, but she would be happy to see what I had to say. I was interested in her reaction to the suggestion that we should pass a federal law against spanking children. She shared the following anecdote with me.

"While I was cooking dinner one afternoon, my three-year-old Jenny was in the family room watching *Sesame Street*. I peeked in to check on her, and she was nowhere in sight, but the sliding glass door leading to the backyard was wide open. I ran outside to find her, but I couldn't see her. I was in a panic. While screaming for her, I went to a neighbor for help so that we could look in different directions. A parent's worst nightmare. She was in none of the sur-rounding yards. I knocked on a second neighbor's door for more help, figuring that the more people that knew she was missing, the greater our chances of finding her. A few minutes later, someone yelled that they had found her. She was a few houses down, playing inside of an open garage.

"I explained to her that she should always ask Mom or Dad before she goes outside and told her about getting lost, kidnapped, or hit by a car.

"I tried to watch her more closely, but still found her outside on the deck the next day. I again explained the problems of getting lost, stolen, or injured and gave her time-out. A third time, I found her unlocking and then stepping out of the front door. I said, 'No, no Jenny, you cannot go outside without asking Mom or Dad,' and gave her a tap-tap on the behind. There was no pain involved, but for a few seconds she shed tears. She seemed to realize the serious-ness of the issue and this was the last occurrence."

Sandy went on to explain to me that she didn't think this would be an appropriate way for a parent to respond to a child over three, who should be able to comprehend the seriousness of her behavior. She told me that she didn't consider this to have been a spanking (even though I—or an onlooking neighbor—might). She said that she thought it would be ludicrous to call what she did a criminal act or even an act that is harmful to the child. She agrees that we should be careful not to let abuse be masked in the name of discipline, that we should educate the public about the problems with spanking and alternative approaches to discipline, that we should make corporal punishment illegal in the schools and insti-tutions and socially unacceptable at home, but she believes that making spanking illegal is an extremist's view.

I agree with Sandy's basic philosophy of parenting. Like many parents, she did not consider what she did to Jenny to really be a spanking. Many parents, in a similar situation, after finding their child, would have surely administered a more severe spanking. Although Sandy stated that she was not angry and did not lose con-trol, that is a difficult feat in such a situation. Even those who rarely spank can lose control because of the anger, frustration, and guilt caused by the kind of potentially dangerous incident that she described. However, if I had talked with her after the first incident of her child leaving the house, I would have suggested some simple ecological solutions. She could have installed a rod in the sliding door to prevent its opening without removal of the rod and a simple device on the front door so that Jenny could not open the door by herself. Also, because this was a potentially dangerous behavior, I would have suggested time-out immediately following the first incident. Further, Sandy could have set up a reward system for short periods of time that Jenny did not try to go outside on her own.

I realize that it is impossible for parents to consult a psychologist every time a minor disciplinary problem occurs. It is obvious that Sandy was able to handle the situation in a manner that was satisfactory to her, but my point is that *there are always alternatives to the spanking*. The more parents like Sandy read and learn about discipline, the less they may think that abolishing spanking is an extremist's solution. I hope this book will convince other enlightened parents like Sandy that it is impossible to legislate a nationally acceptable line between "nonpainful" spanking, "normal" spanking, beating, and abuse.

Like Sandy, I too am afraid when big government interferes in personal decisions. I do not want government officials telling me what to read, telling me what I can view, getting between me and my doctor's medical decisions, or allowing businesses to use my social security number to track my life. However, I believe that government is responsible for protecting children, who can not protect themselves. We already have many federal laws that protect children within their families. I am just suggesting one more, not because I want to see the development of a National Police Force to Arrest Spankers, but because such a law would begin to change people's attitudes about spanking and abuse. It's possible. Let's take a look at how some other Western democracies have fared under such laws.

The Swedish Example

Prior to the Second World War, Sweden was a poor, agrarian, authoritarian country, dominated by fundamentalist religious dogma. By 1979, punitive religious mandates in parenting were on the wane. However, even though corporal punishment had been banned in the schools in 1958, parental use of severe spankings resulted in unacceptable rates of child abuse. In fact, in the early 1970s, 18 percent of all child deaths in Sweden were due to family violence. A study conducted in 1965 indicated that 53 percent of Swedish citizens believed that spanking was necessary. Although this figure dropped to 35 percent in 1971, the change in opinion apparently did not significantly reduce child abuse.

Because of the growing influence of female legislators who were family oriented and as the result of work by child advocates and a government report, in 1979 Sweden passed a law banning the spanking of children. The purpose of the law was to stop beatings and encourage parenting based on nurturance and prevention. *The law did not carry any penalties.* And even though over the years spiteful neighbors or angry children have reported minor offenses, no one has ever been arrested. However, children and other citizens have reported substantial cases of child abuse, and that is still an offense that is prohibited and may carry penalties. So what are the results of this law, which many Americans would consider a horrible intrusion on the rights of the family?

In 1981, only 26 percent of parents supported spanking. The support rate is currently less than 11 percent. According to Joan Durrant, professor of family studies at the University of Manitoba in Canada, Sweden went from a family violence–related child death rate of 18 percent in 1970 to 0 percent in recent years.

Dr. Adrienne Haeuser, professor emeritus of social work at the University of Wisconsin at Milwaukee, is an expert on the effects of Sweden's antispanking law. She completed comparative studies in 1981 and 1988 and found dramatic changes in parental discipline styles. The rapid change from an authoritarian society to one based on equity and social democracy led many child guidance experts to promote a level of permissiveness that was ill advised. This early permissiveness, which was abandoned by the 1980s, has given Sweden a bad rap and has been associated with real and imagined ills by conservative Americans.

In Dr. Haeuser's 1988 follow-up study, she found parents were universally setting limits, using persuasion, negotiation, and conflict resolution techniques, and insisting on eye contact between parent and child, even if this meant holding a child firmly to focus attention while discussing proper behavior.

It is clear from the research of Durrant, Haeuser, and others who have studied Sweden that Swedish families are flourishing. The antispanking bill was only one stage in the evolution of a society that is basically nonviolent and cares about families. This care has translated into legislation that has protected and nurtured the family through economic and social incentives such as extensive family leave policies and the provision of adequate day care for young children. So—what is so bad about a law that reflects these values?

According to the international organization, EPOCH—Worldwide (End Physical Punishment of Children—Worldwide, headquartered in England), the Swedish law has been adapted by Norway, Finland, Denmark, Cyprus, and Austria. As this book is being written, Germany is considering a draft of a similar bill. Switzerland, Poland, Spain, Croatia, Ireland, Canada, and New Zealand are countries in which government commissions and advocacy groups are also pushing their legislatures toward the abolishment of corporal punishment.

The Italian Example

On May 16, 1996, the Supreme Court of Italy issued a decision prohibiting parents from using corporal punishment to discipline their children. The case began when Natalino Cambria was charged with mistreatment of a child when he repeatedly kicked and beat his ten-year-old daughter, Danila, for lying, getting bad grades, and other minor misdeeds. He was convicted in a lower court and appealed the conviction to the Italian Supreme Court. His defense was that he meant to correct her behavior rather than maltreat her. He did not intend to cause danger, injury, or death.

The Italian Supreme Court upheld the conviction and held that Cambria had violated Italy's statutory prohibition against mistreating children. Judge Francisco Ippolito, who wrote the opinion for the court, said in an interview with Susan Bitensky, a professor of law at Michigan State University, that the court wanted to use this case to establish the legal principle that parents in Italy are barred from using any corporal punishment to discipline their children. The court said that "the use of violence for educational purposes can no longer be considered lawful."

The Supreme Court held that parental use of corporal punishment is inconsistent with the established Italian law. First, the Italian Constitution and family laws state that minors are to be treated with the same dignity as adults. Second, the Italian Constitution repudiates the use of violence to solve problems. Third, Italy was a party to the UN Convention on the Rights of the Child, and the resulting treaty holds that children have a right to the harmonious development of their personality and should be raised in a spirit of peace and with tolerance.

An English Case

In February 1993, a stepfather was arrested for beating his stepchild with a stick. During the trial, the judge charged the jury with conflicting information. He admitted that an adult who hit another adult, thereby causing bodily injury, bruising, and swelling, would be convicted. But because similar damage occurred to a child and because the stepfather was merely attempting to correct the boy in a "moderate" manner by repeated canings, it was a different case. The jury acquitted the stepfather, but a group of child advocates in England appealed to the European Commission of Human Rights. This appeal was based on the fact that England had signed the UN Convention on the Rights of the Child, which obliges signatories to protect children from physical violence while in the care of parents and others.

The European Commission on Human Rights ruled that the case was admissible and agreed to consider its merits. As I write this book, the commission is negotiating with the English government to promote a friendly settlement. If this does not occur, the case could be referred the European Court of Human Rights. If this court were to uphold the rights of the child in this case, it is possible that all countries under the jurisdiction of this court would have to ban spanking.

What Can You Do?

In concluding this book, I would like to make some suggestions. Whether or not you agree with me that spanking should be banned, if you have read this whole book, I believe that you understand that it is not really necessary. So the best thing that you can do is to continue to improve your own disciplinary procedures. It will be helpful for you to identify whether you feel more comfortable using extrinsic or intrinsic techniques or a combination of all of the methods I have described. At the end, I have provided further resources so that you can explore particular approaches in depth.

I believe that the better you become at discipline, the more likely you are to help yourself and your friends and relatives to understand some of the simple and complex causes of misbehavior. You will appreciate the value of prevention and understand the futility of physical punishment.

If you choose to join in the struggle against spanking in America, I invite you to contact me personally, through NCSCPA at Temple University. (The address and telephone number appear on the first page of the Resources.) NCSCPA and I can provide you with more extensive information, including materials about the international organization EPOCH and its American chapters.

Resources and Further Reading

My intention in writing this book was to make a highly readable summary of the case against spanking. Unlike most of my writings, this one tries not to impede the reader with a clutter of citations, footnotes, and references in the text. If you are interested in any of the sources I mention, you will find most of them among the following books and articles. This list is by no means meant to be exhaustive; if you wish a more extensive reference list you may obtain it from the NCSCPA. Request the *Publication List* from NCSCPA, 255 RHA Temple University, Philadelphia, PA 19122; phone 215–204–6091; fax 215–204–6013; e-mail ncscpa@blue.vm.temple.edu. I have organized a bibliography under major categories.

The following selection of texts on developmental stages and positive discipline represents only a small percentage of books available. Inclusion here does not imply my endorsement of these books over the multitude of other titles available; it often simply means that the book in question was analyzed as part of our research.

Punitiveness, Psychological Maltreatment, Corporal Punishment, and Prevention

Altemeyer, B. (1988). *Enemies of freedom: Understanding right-wing authoritarianism*. San Francisco: Jossey-Bass.

Anthony, E., & Kohler, B. (Eds.). (1987). *The invulnerable child*. New York: Guilford Press.

Axelrod, S., & Apsche, J. (Eds.). (1984). *The effects of punishment on human behavior*. Orlando: Academic Press.

Baron, R. A., & Richardson, D. R. (1994). *Human aggression* (2nd ed.). New York: Plenum.

Brassard, M., Germain, R., & Hart, S. (Eds.). (1987). *Psychological maltreatment of children and youth*. New York: Pergamon Press.

Dreyer, S. S. (1977). *The bookfinder: A guide to children's literature about the needs and problems of youth aged 2–15*. Circle Pines, MN: American Guidance Service.

Dreyer, S. S. (1989). *The bookfinder 4: When kids need books*. Circle Pines, MN: American Guidance Service.

Dreyer, S. S. (1992). *The best of bookfinder: Selected titles from volumes 1–3*. Circle Pines, MN: American Guidance Service.

Garbarino, J., Guttman, E., & Seeley, J. (1986). *The psychologically battered child*. San Francisco: Jossey-Bass.

Gibson, I. (1978). *The English vice*. London: Duckworth.

Graziano, A. M. (1992). Why we should study sub-abusive violence against children. *The Child, Youth, and Family Services Quarterly, 15* (4), 6–8.

Graziano, A., & Namaste, K. (1990). Parental use of physical force in child discipline: A survey of 679 college students. *Journal of Interpersonal Violence, 5,* 449–463.

Greven, P. (1980). *The Protestant temperament*. New York: Knopf.

Greven, P. (1991). *Spare the child: The religious roots of punishment and the psychological impact of physical abuse*. New York: Knopf.

Haeuser, A. (1992). Swedish parents don't spank. *Mothering, 63,* 42–49.

Hyman, I. A. (1990). *Reading, writing and the hickory stick: The appalling story of physical and psychological abuse in American schools*. San Francisco: New Lexington Press.

Hyman, I. A. (1995). Corporal punishment, psychological maltreatment, violence, and punitiveness in America: Research, advocacy, and public policy. *Applied & Preventive Psychology, 4,* 113–130.

Hyman, I. A., Clarke, J., & Erdlen, R. (1987). An analysis of physical abuse in American schools. *Aggressive Behavior, 13,* 1–7.

Hyman, I. A., & Wise, J. (1979). *Corporal punishment in American education*. Philadelphia: Temple University Press.

Kelder, L. R., McNamara, J. R., Carlson, B., & Lynn, S. J. (1991). Perceptions of physical punishment: The relation to childhood and adolescent experiences. *Journal of Interpersonal Violence, 6* (4), 432–445.

Kohn, A. (1990). *The brighter side of human nature: Altruism and empathy in everyday life.* New York: Basic Books.

McCord, J. (1988). Parental behavior in the cycle of aggression. *Psychiatry, 51,* 14–23.

Miller, A. (1983). *For your own good.* New York: Farrar, Straus & Giroux.

National Committee for the Prevention of Child Abuse. (1991). Public attitudes and behaviors with respect to child abuse prevention, 1987–1991. Chicago: Author.

Pinel, J.P.J. (1993). *Biopsychology* (2nd ed.). Needham Heights, MA: Allyn & Bacon.

Power, T., & Chapieski, M. (1986). Childrearing and impulse control in toddlers: A naturalistic investigation. *Developmental Psychology, 22* (2), 271–275.

Straus, M. A. (1994). *Beating the devil out of them: Corporal punishment in American families.* San Francisco: New Lexington Press.

Wiehe, E. (1990). Religious influence of parental attitudes toward the use of corporal punishment. *Journal of Family Violence, 5,* 173–186.

Weiss, B., Dodge, K. A., Bates, J. E., & Pettit, G. S. (1992). Some consequences of early harsh discipline: Child aggression and a maladaptive social information processing style. *Child Development, 63,* 1321–1335.

Appropriate Developmental Behavior

Ames, L. B., & Ilg, F. L. (1976). *Your two year old child.* New York: Dell. (This is one of a series with different books for different age levels.)

Caplan, F., & Caplan, T. (1990). *The second twelve months of life.* New York: Bantam Books.

Caplan, F., & Caplan, T. (1995). *The first twelve months of life.* New York: Bantam Books.

Caplan, T., & Caplan, F. (1984). *The early childhood years: The 2 to 6 year old.* New York: Bantam Books.

Renshaw J. K. (1994). *Positive parenting from A to Z.* New York: Ballantine.

Spock, B., & Rothenberg, M. B. (1992). *Dr. Spock's baby and child care.* New York: Pocket Books.

Positive Discipline

Aetna Life and Casualty Company. (1992). *Resolving conflicts through mediation*. Hartford, CT: Author.

Albert, L. (1989). *Cooperative discipline*. Circle Pines, MN: American Guidance Service.

Alberto, P., & Troutman, A. (1990). *Applied behavior analysis for teachers* (3rd ed.). Columbus, OH: Merrill.

Bash, M., & Camp, B. (1985). *Think aloud*. Champaign, IL: Research Press.

Canter, L., & Canter, M. (1992). *Assertive discipline* (Rev. ed.). Santa Monica, CA: Lee Canter & Associates.

Cartledge, G., & Milburn, J. (1986). *Teaching social skills to children* (2nd ed.). Needham Heights, MA: Allyn & Bacon.

Curwin, R., & Mendler, A. (1988). *Discipline with dignity*. Alexandria, VA: Association for Supervision and Curriculum Development.

Deutsch-Smith, D., & Rivera, D. (1993). *Effective discipline*. Austin, TX: PRO-ED.

Dinkmeyer, D., McKay, G., & Dinkmeyer, D., Jr. (1980). *Systematic training for effective teaching (STET)*. Circle Pines, MN: American Guidance Service.

Dupont, H., Gardner, O., & Brody, D. (1974). *Toward effective development (TAD)*. Circle Pines, MN: American Guidance Service.

Elias, M., & Clabby, J. (1989). *Social decision making skills*. Rockville, MD: Aspen.

Elliot, S., & Gresham, F. (1991). *Social skills intervention guide*. Circle Pines, MN: American Guidance Service.

Ellsworth, J., & Monahan, A. (1987). *A humanistic approach to teaching and learning through developmental discipline*. New York: Irvington.

Faber, A., & Mazish, E. (1982). *How to talk so kids will listen and listen so kids will talk*. New York: Avon Books.

Fine, M. (1994). A systems-ecological perspective on home-school intervention. In M. Fine & C. Carlson (Eds.), *The handbook of family-school intervention: A systems perspective*. Needham Heights, MA: Allyn & Bacon.

Jackson, N., Jackson, D., & Monroe, C. (1983). *Getting along with others*. Champaign, IL: Research Press.

Goldstein, A., Glick, B., Reiner, S., Zimmerman, D., & Coultry, T. (1987). *Aggression replacement training*. Champaign, IL: Research Press.

Goldstein, A., Spafkin, R., Gershaw, N., & Klein, P. (1980). *Skillstreaming the adolescent*. Champaign, IL: Research Press.

Good Shepherd Neighborhood House Mediation Program. (1993). *Student mediators training manual*. Philadelphia: Author.

Gordon, T. (1991). *Discipline that works: Promoting self-discipline in children*. New York: Plume-Penguin.

Hyman, I. A., Dahbany, A., Blum, M., Weiler, E., & Brooks-Klein, V. (1996). *School discipline and school violence: The teacher variance approach*. Needham Heights, MA: Allyn & Bacon.

Jackson, N., Jackson, D., & Monroe, C. (1983). *Getting along with others*. Champaign, IL: Research Press.

Johnson, D., & Johnson, R. (1991). *Learning together and alone*. Needham Heights, MA: Allyn & Bacon.

Kaplan, J., & Drainville, B. (1991). *Beyond behavior modification*. Austin, TX: PRO-ED.

Keating, B., Pickering, M., Slack, B., & White, J. (1990). *A guide to positive discipline*. Needham Heights, MA: Allyn & Bacon.

Kersey, K. (1990). *Don't take it out on your kids: A parent's and teacher's guide to positive discipline*. Washington, DC: Acropolis Books.

Mannix, D. (1986). *I can behave*. Austin, TX: PRO-ED.

McGinnis, E., & Goldstein, A. (1990). *Skillstreaming in early childhood*. Champaign, IL: Research Press.

Page, P., & Cieloha, D. (1990). *Getting along: A social skills program*. Circle Pines, MN: American Guidance Service.

Painter, G., & Corsini, R. (1990). *Effective discipline in the home and school*. Muncie, IN: Accelerated Development.

Rath, L., Harmin, M., & Simon, S. B. (1978). *Values and teaching* (2nd ed.). Columbus, OH: Merrill.

Sabatino, D., Sabatino, A., & Mann, L. (1983). *Discipline and behavioral management*. Rockville, MD: Aspen.

Sadalla, G., Holmberg, M., & Haligan, J. (1990). *Conflict resolution: An elementary school curriculum*. San Francisco: Community Board.

Savage, T. (1991). *Discipline for self control*. Needham Heights, MA: Allyn & Bacon.

Schrumpt, F., Crawford, D., & Usadel, H. (1991). *Peer mediation*. Champaign, IL: Research Press.

Schumaker, J., Hazek, J., & Pederson, C. (1988). *Social skills for daily living*. Circle Pines, MN: American Guidance Service.

Shure, M. (1992). *I can problem solve (ICPS)*. Champaign, IL: Research Press.

Vernon, A. (1989). *Thinking, feeling, behaving*. Champaign, IL: Research Press.

Waksman, S., Messmer, C., & Waksman, D. (1988). *The Waksman social skills curriculum* (3rd ed.). Austin, TX: PRO-ED.

Wood, M., & Long, N. (1991). *Life space intervention*. Austin, TX: PRO-ED.

The Author

Irwin A. Hyman, director of the National Center for the Study of Corporal Punishment and Alternatives and professor of school psychology at Temple University, is an accomplished scholar, researcher, and practitioner who is recognized internationally for his work on corporal punishment and discipline. He is a fellow of the American Psychological Association and of the International Society for Research on Aggression and a diplomate in school and clinical psychology—American Board of Professional Psychology.

Dr. Hyman is coeditor of the definitive text *Corporal Punishment in American Education*, author of *Reading, Writing and the Hickory Stick: The Appalling Story of Physical and Psychological Abuse in American Schools*, with a foreword by Phil Donahue, and *School Discipline and School Violence: The Teacher Variance Approach*, in addition to over a hundred other articles and publications. He has appeared frequently in the media, including appearances on *Donahue*, *Today*, *Good Morning America*, *Sally Jessy Raphael*, *Geraldo*, and *Oprah*. He has been quoted in most of the major newspapers and news magazines in America, and has testified before Congress and state legislatures.

Index